COUNTERING
THE NEW
TERRORISM

Ian O. Lesser ■ Bruce Hoffman
John Arquilla ■ David Ronfeldt ■ Michele Zanini
Foreword by Brian Michael Jenkins

Prepared for the
United States Air Force

RAND
Project AIR FORCE

FOREWORD

Brian Michael Jenkins

RAND's research on terrorism formally began in 1972. Two bloody terrorist incidents that year—the Japanese Red Army attack on passengers at the Lod Airport in Israel and the seizure of Israeli athletes by Black September terrorists at the Olympics in Munich—signaled dramatically to the world that a new mode of warfare had begun. Reacting to this new threat, then President Nixon created the Cabinet Committee to Combat Terrorism, a high-level group to coordinate all U.S. counterterrorist efforts. The committee in turn commissioned RAND to examine the phenomenon and how it might affect American security interests.

Terrorism was not a new concern for the government, at least in its particular forms—the hijacking of airliners, the kidnapping of diplomats, protest bombings. However, as is so often the case, dramatic events focused interest and mobilized resources. Nor was this entirely new territory for RAND, which previously had studied the use of terrorism in revolutionary and guerrilla warfare, already had identified the new phenomenon of urban guerrilla warfare and its inherent tendency toward the employment of terrorist tactics, and had examined the problem of airline hijackings and assassinations.

Having been present at the initiation of RAND's research on terrorism, and now 27 years later being called upon to review this latest RAND volume, *Countering the New Terrorism*, by Ian Lesser and his colleagues, provides me an opportunity for review and reflection, as well as for pointing out some of the unanticipated consequences of our endeavor.

When we began our research, we thought that terrorism, in its contemporary form, reflected a unique confluence of political events and technological developments that made it likely to increase and become increasingly international, and that it would affect the interests of the United States and its allies in a variety of ways, but we had only a dim notion of terrorism's spectacular future. Indeed, anyone at the beginning of the 1970s who forecast that terrorists would blow up jumbo jets in mid-air with all of their passengers on board, crash a hijacked airliner into a city, kidnap a head of state, run a boat filled with explosives aground on a crowded beach, set off a bomb weighing several tons in the heart of London's financial district or blow up the World Trade Center in New York, release nerve gas in a subway at rush hour, unleash biological weapons, or hold a city hostage with a stolen or improvised nuclear weapon would have been dismissed as a novelist.

Yet of the nine possible events described here, four have occurred and four more have been attempted or at least threatened. Terrorists have blown up airliners; they have set off huge bombs in the heart of London and at the World Trade Center in New York; and they have released nerve gas in a Tokyo subway. Terrorists have plotted to crash a hijacked airliner into a city and attempted to beach an explosives-laden boat in Israel in an effort to kill hundreds of swimmers, and deranged individuals have threatened to use biological and nuclear weapons. Only the abduction of a head of state remains in the realm of fiction, but only because Aldo Moro, five times Italy's prime minister, happened not to be the premier when he was kidnapped and murdered by terrorists in 1978. Today's lurid speculations turn into tomorrow's headlines, making it hard to dismiss even the most far-fetched scenarios. That creates an analytical problem: How do we assess the threat of terrorist events that have not occurred? Why have terrorists not done some of the things we know they are capable of doing? What we do know is that the terrorist threat today differs greatly from that of a quarter century ago. Terrorism evolves, which is one of the major themes of this volume.

One of our first tasks in 1972 was to construct a chronology of terrorist incidents to provide an empirical foundation for the subject of our research. When we talked about terrorism, what exactly were we talking about? The selection of entries for inclusion in the chronology required defining terrorism, ideally, in an objective manner. To avoid distracting polemics about who was a terrorist or whether ends justified means, it was necessary to define terrorism according to the quality of the act, not the identity of the perpetrator or the nature of the cause. In separating terrorist tactics from their political context, the intent clearly was to criminalize a certain mode of political expression or warfare.

We concluded that an act of terrorism was first of all a crime in the classic sense such as murder or kidnapping, albeit for political motives. Even if we accepted the assertion by many terrorists that they were waging war and were therefore soldiers—that is, privileged combatants in the strict legal sense—terrorist tactics, in most cases, violated the rules that governed armed conflict—for example, the deliberate targeting of noncombatants or actions against hostages. We recognized that terrorism contained a psychological component—it was aimed at the people watching. The identities of the actual targets or victims of the attack often were secondary or irrelevant to the terrorists' objective of spreading fear and alarm or gaining concessions. This separation between the actual victim of the violence and the target of the intended psychological effect was the hallmark of terrorism. It was by no means a perfect definition and it certainly did not end any debates, but it offered some useful distinctions between terrorism and ordinary crime, other forms of armed conflict, or the acts of psychotic individuals.

Defining terrorism according to the act would closely resemble the approach followed by the international community. Unable to agree upon a universal definition of terrorism, states were nonetheless able to reach a measure of consensus in outlawing specific acts such as airline hijacking and aircraft sabotage, attacks on diplomats, or the taking of hostages. In making these specific actions international crimes, the word "terrorism" was seldom used; collectively, however, the acts constituted terrorism, which then was universally condemned.

The creation of the RAND chronology, although a prerequisite to empirical research, lent greater coherence to a spattering of disparate acts of violence than what was offered by the terrorists themselves, few of whom at the time thought of assassinations, bombings, kidnappings, and airline hijackings as elements of a unified tactical repertoire, let alone the basis of a strategy. Ironically, in our effort to understand a phenomenon, we ran the risk of attributing to terrorists a level of strategic thinking they may not have possessed.

Our definitional approach also may have had another unanticipated consequence. Terrorists were defined as those who carried out certain acts defined as terrorism.

While perfectly logical, this definition risked becoming an analytically constraining tautology. When those already identified as terrorists did something different, it would correctly be seen as a tactical innovation. (As a matter of fact, terrorists turned out not to be very innovative; instead, they tended to stick with a limited tactical repertoire.) But what if tactical developments came from another entirely different dimension? For example, those to first use nerve gas on a civilian population were not "terrorists," but members of a bizarre religious cult. Looking ahead to possible assaults on information networks—so-called "cyberwar," which is discussed by John Arquilla, David Ronfeldt, and Michele Zanini in this volume—if we focus exclusively on whether existing terrorists will switch from bombing to hacking, we may find few examples. However, other kinds of adversaries may move in the direction of mass disruption through the penetration and sabotage of information networks. Terrorists might not become hackers, but increasingly malevolent hackers could become a new kind of white-collar terrorist.

We defined *international terrorism* as encompassing those acts in which the terrorists crossed national frontiers to carry out attacks, or attacked foreign targets at home such as embassies or international lines of commerce as in airline hijackings. This focus reflected initial fascination with the novelty of contemporary terrorism's international character. How did it come about in the Lod Airport massacre, people asked, that Japanese terrorists came to Israel on behalf of Palestinians to kill passengers on an inbound U.S. flight, most of whom happened to be Puerto Rican pilgrims visiting the Holy Land?

Defining "international terrorism" was a necessary prerequisite for mobilizing international support against terrorism and could be viewed as a noble effort to extend the international rule of law— international efforts against piracy provided an historical precedent—and the conventions governing war. It also served U.S. national interests in that the principal terrorist threat to the United States came not from terrorist attacks inside the United States but rather from terrorist attacks on American citizens and facilities abroad. The chronology of international terrorism reinforced this concern by showing that U.S. citizens and facilities were the number one target in international incidents of terrorism. The United States had no mandate to intervene in the internal conflicts of other nations, but when that violence spilled over into the international community, it became a legitimate international concern.

These definitional constructions enabled us to initiate a long-term analysis of terrorism that RAND has continued to the present day. The annual chronologies have illustrated trends in terrorist tactics, changes in the patterns of targeting, motives, lethality, and other developments which, in turn, provided useful information about the effectiveness of various countermeasures. Over the long run, they showed that physical security measures worked—the frequency of terrorist attacks declined where targets were hardened, but terrorists merely shifted their sights to other, softer targets. Terrorists gradually, but never entirely, abandoned tactics that proved increasingly unproductive and dangerous, such as embassy takeovers. The lethality of terrorist attacks gradually increased over time as terrorists motivated by ethnic hatreds or religious fanaticism revealed themselves to be demonstrably less constrained, more inclined to carry out large-scale indiscriminate attacks. All these conclusions, now commonplace in our knowledge, came out of the simple quantitative analysis made possible by the data assembled. Bruce Hoffman, in his chapter, demonstrates the utility of this type of analysis.

However, quantitative analysis could easily be pushed too far. The effort to be objective and precise created necessarily artificial categories. One has to remember that international terrorist incidents constitute only a narrowly defined component of all terrorist incidents, which in some cases comprised all of the political violence taking place in a country—so called "pure terrorism," but in other cases comprised only a small component of a much larger conflict. In civil war situations, like that in Lebanon, separating incidents of terrorism from the background of violence and bloodshed was both futile and meaningless. Measuring the volume of international terrorism—the thickness of a thin crust atop a very deep pie—would tell us little about the root causes of terrorism or the nature of societies that produced terrorists.

There is anyway a dangerous tendency to attribute the actions of a few to the political defects or cultural flaws of the society as a whole. True, terrorists are not extraterrestrials. They arise from the peculiarities of local situations, although they may become isolated in their own tiny universe of beliefs and discourse that is completely alien to their surrounding society. We also must recognize that there are those for whom the banner of a cause offers an excuse for individual aggression—terrorists for whom terrorism is an end in itself. In a world in which terrorism has so thoroughly permeated the popular culture, providing inspiration and instruction for acting out in certain prescribed ways, terrorists who are mere thugs with political pretensions, psychopaths seeking notoriety, or ordinary crackpots are becoming a more prevalent threat.

RAND's research remained pragmatic. It delved into the mind-set of terrorists but avoided the depths of psychodynamics. RAND's political analysts provided expertise on the various countries and regions where terrorist groups were active, but spent little time looking for a lodestone of political or economic conditions that produced terrorism. Instead, RAND focused on what terrorists did, how they did it, and how best to protect society against those actions that could lead to death, widespread disruption, and alarm.

Of immediate concern to the U.S. government when RAND first began its research was the problem of kidnappings. American diplomats already had been kidnapped in Latin America and the Middle East, and the tactic of political kidnapping seemed to be spreading. The U.S. Department of State asked RAND to explore the mechanisms of bargaining for hostage. We began by conducting detailed case studies of the major hostage incidents that had already occurred. From these we were able to distill lessons in how to manage communications with hostage-takers, relations with local governments often thrown into crisis by the event, and other complex aspects of a hostage situation.

As part of the same effort, RAND examined the experiences of those held hostage. This research led to new training for officials assigned to high-risk posts and to greater understanding of the post-release difficulties experienced by hostages. More concretely, it helped bring about a number of specific changes in how returning hostages were treated. Years later, this research was carried into the area of Air Force survival training and the applicability of the military Code of Conduct in cases where personnel were held hostage by terrorists as opposed to conventional prisoner-of-war situations.

The security of American embassies abroad was a major concern. RAND examined the history of embassy takeovers, a terrorist tactic that declined as embassies became better protected and governments became more resistant to terrorists' demands, more skillful in negotiating with terrorists holding hostages, and willing to use force when negotiations failed. RAND also developed a more sophisticated mathematical basis for assessing the risk posed by car bombs, which was used in developing new design and construction criteria for U.S. embassies.

If terrorists could blow up airliners and assault embassies, might they not also attempt to steal nuclear weapons to hold cities hostage or seize nuclear facilities and threaten catastrophic damage? In the mid-1970s, amid growing concerns about the possibility of nuclear terrorism, the U.S. Department of Energy and Sandia Laboratories asked RAND to analyze the motives and capabilities of potential malevolent adversaries of U.S. nuclear programs—a deliberately broad label that could include terrorists, economically motivated criminals, deranged individuals, and other foes. The approach in this research differed from the analysis of terrorist kidnappings or embassy takeovers in that, fortunately for society, we did not have a rich history of serious events of nuclear terrorism to examine. Instead, RAND looked at the combinations of motives and capabilities displayed in analogous events: the most ambitious terrorist attacks, wartime commando raids, high-value heists, incidents of industrial sabotage, and the careers of mad bombers. These analog case studies provided useful insights and suggested a security strategy: Nuclear security systems would strive to compel attackers to possess combinations of dedication, know-how, and resources not previously seen outside of national wartime efforts. The Department of Energy later credited RAND with having designed the threat upon which its security programs were based.

One offshoot of this inquiry was the development of an arsenal of techniques to assess the credibility of threats made by persons or groups claiming to have nuclear material or homemade nuclear bombs. While most such threats, of which there were a growing number in the late 1970s, could easily be dismissed as the obvious products of pranksters or lunatics, their quality was improving as the theoretical knowledge of nuclear weapons design spread and novels about nuclear terrorism—some well-informed—proliferated. Nuclear terrorism became part of popular culture. Remote behavioral analysis techniques were explored, refined, and tested against actual threats, in many cases providing direct assistance to law enforcement. The same analytical techniques were later utilized to examine the mind-set of terrorists and others threatening violence or engaged in murderous campaigns. In the years since, these profiling techniques have become a routine facet of criminal investigations.

Will tomorrow's terrorist simply be a more bloodthirsty version of today's terrorist bent upon big bangs and body count, perhaps even more indiscriminate, but sticking with conventional explosives? Will tomorrow's terrorist turn instead to chemical, biological, or nuclear weapons to cause mass destruction? Or will tomorrow's terrorist be a sophisticated electronic warrior penetrating and sabotaging the information and communications systems upon which modern society increasingly depends? *Countering the New Terrorism* explores these dimensions, and one in particular, the possibility of netwar.

While no one can predict the future course of terrorism with confidence, the history of terrorism counsels us to think broadly but at the same time to exercise caution. The analysis of "dream threats" is filled with pitfalls. It is easy to begin by identifying vulnerabilities—they are infinite, positing theoretical adversaries— they are legion, then reifying the threat—a subtle shift of verbs from *could* to *may* happen. "Could" means theoretically possible while "may" suggests more. So long as the reader and the policymakers understand the utility of what necessarily must be speculative, there is no problem. The danger arises when speculation becomes the basis for launching costly efforts to prevent "what ifs," or worse, when policymakers believe that highly publicized preventive or mitigation efforts will deter such adversaries. This is not to say the threat is not real. I believe that major assaults on information systems are a real possibility. Terrorist use of chemical or biological weapons is a legitimate concern, although the evidence here is sketchier. My intention is rather to point to the risks of fact-free analysis.

While the bulk of RAND's research focused on understanding the terrorist adversary, RAND also addressed many aspects of response. Identifying negotiating tactics used successfully in hostage situations is one obvious example. RAND also carried out several studies in the area of intelligence collection, analysis, and dissemination. One project developed a framework for collecting and analyzing information about terrorist groups. Another study tackled the sensitive issue of the impact of new constraints, which had been imposed on domestic intelligence-gathering beginning in the late 1970s, on the ability of authorities to prevent acts of terrorism and apprehend terrorists. By studying the intelligence-collection techniques that had been used successfully under the old rules, then applying the new constraints, RAND's research did show that there had been a significant impact. Many of the old successes could not have been repeated under the new rules. However, despite the increased limitations on intelligence-gathering, the volume of domestic terrorism in the United States had declined for broader social and political reasons. Hence, the tradeoff between the threat terrorists posed to society and the civil liberties that the increased constraints were intended to protect seemed tolerable. Clearly, however, investigations of "terrorist" activity moved from preventive to reactive.

This issue arises again as we contemplate the possibilities of terrorist use of weapons of mass destruction. The record of terrorist apprehension in the United States is a very good one, but faced with a credible threat of mass destruction, a frightened population will demand prevention, which in a panic situation could imperil civil liberties. The likelihood of overreaction increases if the authorities have absolutely no sources of intelligence. The challenge is to strike the balance between prudence and paranoia. How? Research can make people smart, but not wise.

It is reassuring to see occasional arrests of individuals plotting to carry out terrorist actions, albeit on lesser charges of weapons possession or conspiracy. Although inherently difficult to prosecute, such cases demonstrate that intelligence capabilities are not entirely moribund.

Should the United States deal with terrorism as crime or as a mode of warfare? The two concepts have entirely different operational implications. If terrorism is considered a criminal matter, we are concerned with gathering evidence, correctly determining the culpability of the individuals responsible for a particular act, and apprehending and bringing the perpetrators to trial.

Dealing with terrorism as a criminal matter, however, presents a number of problems. Evidence is extremely difficult to gather in an international investigation where all countries might not cooperate with the investigators. Apprehending terrorists abroad is also difficult. Moreover, the criminal approach does not provide an entirely satisfactory response to a continuing campaign of terrorism waged by a distant group, and it may not work against a state sponsor of terrorism.

If, on the other hand, we view terrorism as war, we are less concerned with individual culpability. Proximate responsibility—for example, correct identification of the terrorist group—will do. We may be less fastidious about evidence: It need not be of courtroom quality; intelligence reporting will suffice. The focus is not on the accused individual but on the correct identification of the *enemy*.

A military response demonstrates resolves, reassures wavering allies, galvanizes other governments to action, and can temporarily disrupt terrorist operations. Whether military force is an effective deterrent is problematical. Military force also has its drawbacks. It can result in friendly casualties and the death of innocent bystanders; it can create terrorist martyrs and provoke retaliation; it can alienate world public opinion and reduce international cooperation; and declaring war on terrorist leaders puts the United States into open-ended asymmetrical contests.

The utility of military force as a response to terrorism has been debated in government since the early 1980s, and has been discussed in several RAND publications. Ian Lesser tackles the subject again in the present volume, focusing on the role of the Air Force, which is appropriate, given the U.S. government's preference for air power and cruise missiles as the weapon of choice. Lesser's key contribution is the development of a strategic framework for assessing counterterrorism efforts—something not previously done.

One can be critical. Over a quarter century of research, yet terrorism persists. It is because terrorism is not a problem that awaits a solution but rather, as *Countering the New Terrorism* emphasizes, it is a changing threat. There is still much to be done.

Terrorism has become an increasingly dangerous threat to U.S. security. U.S. officials now describe it as a "war." We need to further examine the requirements of force protection and the utility of military force as a response to terrorism or to preempt the possible development and use of weapons of mass destruction by terrorists or state actors, an issue underlined by the recent U.S. bombings in Afghanistan and Sudan.

Despite successes in foiling some terrorist attacks and in apprehending individual terrorists, the United States still needs to formulate a clear, realistic, and realizable national strategy that must evolve with a changing terrorist threat, something more than the policy *desiderata* that still pass for policy.

We need to monitor terrorist trends and focus resources on the most likely developments while avoiding costly efforts dictated by peripheral alarms.

Our current arsenal seems inadequate. We need to develop new and more-effective diplomatic tools, and conventional and unconventional ways to combat terrorism. And we need to better integrate counterterrorism with other aspects of U.S. strategy.

Terrorism research is fragmented. Responding effectively to the threat of terrorism requires coordination among numerous government agencies. The machinery and procedures have been created to coordinate the government's response to terrorist incidents, but apart from a committee to review government-sponsored research on terrorism, there is no coordinated research effort.

We need to better understand the underlying conflicts that give rise to terrorism and to systematically exploit the experiences gained by the United States in managing and resolving conflicts that have led to terrorism in the Middle East, Northern Ireland, Bosnia, and Kosovo.

The United States has variously employed sophisticated diplomacy, the manipulation of political and economic payoffs, the threat of force, the application of military power, and monitoring assistance to end terrorist struggles and to prevent new "Palestines." There is much to be learned here. *Countering the New Terrorism,* in my view, makes a significant contribution to our understanding of these issues, but in the enduring task of combating terrorism, it is not likely to be the last installment.

Terrorism is changing, as is its effect on national security. This book brings together three complementary papers that address trends in international terrorism, the special problem of terrorism in the information age, and how to meet the terrorist challenge to U.S. interests. Each of these papers pays special attention to the effect of terrorism on the U.S. military. Each also considers the role of military forces, especially air and space power, in national counterterrorism strategy.

The study made extensive use of the RAND-St. Andrews Chronology of International Terrorism—a comprehensive database on worldwide terrorist incidents since 1968.

The papers were written as contributions to a year-long project on "Terrorism and Counterterrorism: Implications for Strategy and USAF Planning," conducted within the Strategy and Doctrine Program of RAND's Project AIR FORCE. The study was co-sponsored by the Deputy Chief of Staff, Air and Space Operations (AF/XO), and the Director of Intelligence, Surveillance, and Reconnaissance (AF/XOI). It was aimed at helping the Air Force to address its own "force protection" concerns, as well as contributing to the broader national and international debate on terrorism. The findings should be of interest to a wide audience interested in terrorism, counterterrorism, and national security policy.

PROJECT AIR FORCE

Project AIR FORCE, a division of RAND, is the Air Force federally funded research and development center (FFRDC) for studies and analyses. It provides the Air Force with independent analyses of policy alternatives affecting the development, employment, combat readiness, and support of current and future aerospace forces. Research is performed in three programs: Strategy and Doctrine, Force Modernization and Employment, and Resource Management and System Acquisition.

CONTENTS

Foreword
Brian Michael Jenkins   iii

Preface   xv

Figures and Table   xxi

Acknowledgments   xxiii

Chapter One
INTRODUCTION
Ian O. Lesser   1
Changing Terrorism in a Changing World   1
Study Approach and Structure   3

Chapter Two
TERRORISM TRENDS AND PROSPECTS
Bruce Hoffman   7
Introduction   7
Trends In Terrorism   7
Terrorism's Changing Characteristics   8
Terrorism's Increasing Lethality   10
Terrorist Tactical Adaptations Across the Technological
Spectrum and Their Implications   28
Force Protection: The Example of IRA Targeting of
British Forces in Northern Ireland   31
Implications for Antiterrorism and Force Protection . . .   34
Conclusion   35

Chapter Three
  NETWORKS, NETWAR, AND INFORMATION-AGE
    TERRORISM
    John Arquilla, David Ronfeldt, and Michele Zanini . .   39
  A New Terrorism (with Old Roots)   39
  Recent Views About Terrorism   42
  The Advent of Netwar—Analytical Background   45
    Definition of Netwar   47
    More About Organizational Design   48
    Caveats About the Role of Technology   52
    Swarming, and the Blurring of Offense and Defense . . .   53
    Networks Versus Hierarchies: Challenges for
      Counternetwar   55
  Middle Eastern Terrorism and Netwar   56
    Middle Eastern Terrorist Groups: Structure and
      Actions   58
    Middle Eastern Terrorist Groups and the Use of
      Information Technology   64
    Summary Comment   67
  Terrorist Doctrines—The Rise of a "War Paradigm"   68
    The Coercive-Diplomacy Paradigm   68
    The War Paradigm   69
    The New-World Paradigm   71
    The Paradigms and Netwar   71
  Information-Age Terrorism and the U.S. Air Force   72
    Toward a New USAF Strategy for Coping with
      Information-Age Terrorism   74
    Mitigation Measures   75
    Proactive Counterterrorism and the USAF   77
    Targeting Terrorists in the Information Age   80
  Policy Implications and Conclusions for the USAF   81

Chapter Four
  COUNTERING THE NEW TERRORISM: IMPLICATIONS
    FOR STRATEGY
    Ian O. Lesser   85
  Introduction   85
  Understanding and Countering the "New" Terrorism   86
  Terrorism in Strategic Context   88

The Terrorist Threat to U.S. Interests: Four
    Dimensions   88
Direct Threats   88
Indirect Attacks Affecting U.S. Interests   92
Systemic Consequences   93
Terrorism in the War Paradigm   94
Changing Definitions of Security   96
Terrorism and the Conflict Spectrum   97
Future Terrorism Geopolitics   99
Implications for the Future   110
The Lessons and Relevance of Counterterrorism
    Experience.   111
U.S. Experience: A Mixed Legacy   111
The United Kingdom Experience   115
The French Experience   117
The Israeli Experience   120
Allied Perspectives on Terrorist Challenges Facing
    the United States   124
Lessons of the Allied Experience   126
Conceptualizing National Counterterrorism Strategy   126
Core Strategy   127
Environment Shaping   134
Hedging Strategy   138
Conclusions   140
Overall Observations   140
Implications for Military Strategy and the U.S.
    Air Force   142

Index   145

FIGURES AND TABLE

Figures

1. Number of Worldwide Terrorist Incidents,
   1991–1996 11
2. Religious Versus Other Terrorist Groups 16
3. Types of Networks 50

Table

1. USAF Generic Counterterrorism Missions and Policy
   Recommendations 83

ACKNOWLEDGMENTS

The authors wish to express their thanks to the sponsors of this study within the U.S. Air Force for their interest and assistance. The research presented here benefited greatly from the contributions of other members of the RAND study team, including Daniel Byman, Abram Shulsky, David Orletsky, and Maurice Eisenstein. Particular thanks also to RAND colleagues Natalie Crawford, Brian Michael Jenkins, Zalmay Khalilzad, Rosalie Heacock, Jeanne Heller, C. Richard Neu, Alan Vick, and Denise Woerner for their advice, assistance, and support. Our analysis reflects extensive discussions with officials and unofficial observers in the United States and abroad. We are grateful to all those who contributed their views and expertise. Needless to say, any errors or omissions are the responsibility of the authors.

Chapter One

INTRODUCTION

Ian O. Lesser

CHANGING TERRORISM IN A CHANGING WORLD

The last decade has seen extraordinary changes in the international security environment. Decades of Cold War assumptions and strategies have been overthrown, and new debates have emerged on how to explain and address today's more diverse and ambiguous risks. Yet much of the discussion on terrorism remains tied to images drawn from previous epochs. Recent experience, from the bombings of the embassies in Kenya and Tanzania, the World Trade Center, the federal building in Oklahoma City, and Khobar Towers to the use of chemical weapons in the Tokyo subway and Hamas suicide attacks in Israel, has galvanized public and expert attention, and reminds us that terrorism is capable of starkly affecting U.S. citizens and U.S. interests. It also suggests troubling new dimensions, including the potential for terrorist action on U.S. territory and terrorist use of weapons of mass destruction—nuclear, chemical, biological, and radiological.

The old image of a professional terrorist motivated by ideology or the desire for "national liberation," operating according to a specific political agenda, armed with guns and bombs, and backed by overt state sponsors, has not quite disappeared. It has been augmented—some would say overtaken—by other forms of terrorism. This new terrorism has different motives, different actors, different sponsors, and, as Bruce Hoffman discusses in Chapter Two, demonstrably greater lethality. Terrorists are organizing themselves in new, less hierarchical structures and using "amateurs" to a far greater extent than in the past. All of this renders much previous analysis of terrorism based on established groups obsolete, and complicates the task of intelligence-gathering and counterterrorism.

Three points are worth noting as background. First, this study was undertaken for the U.S. Air Force at a time when the attack on the Khobar Towers military housing complex in Dhahran, Saudi Arabia, was fresh in the minds of policymakers, the military, and the public. The Air Force was concerned about understanding the current and future terrorist threat to deployed forces and vigorously addressing the problem of "force protection." Although some aspects of our study treated the problem of close-in defense against terrorist risks to the Air Force, the bulk of our effort was broader, tracing the recent evolution of international terrorism against civilian and U.S. military targets, looking ahead to where terrorism is going, and assessing how it might be contained. We use the term "contained" because, unlike some other security challenges such as nuclear deterrence or the defense of borders, absolute prevention of terrorism is not a realistic objective.

Second, our research was conducted against the background of a wider national debate on aspects of international terrorism, especially the threat of weapons of mass destruction as a prominent "transnational risk." The Defense Science Board and others have examined these risks in detail over the past few years, and recent congressional and National Security Council initiatives have also made this their focus.[1] In addition, it has become fashionable—with some reason—to consider the risk of information-based terrorism. Our study touches on each of these issues, but with less emphasis on the proliferation of technologies and techniques *per se*, and more emphasis on how changes in the sources and nature of terrorism may encourage—or discourage—the use of unconventional terror.

Third, we have been struck by the limited scope of most analyses of contemporary terrorism. Perhaps because the study of the behavior of specific groups was the hallmark of most terrorism research in the recent past, expert analyses of terrorism tend to be just that— analyses of terrorist phenomena with little attempt to characterize

---

[1]See Defense Science Board, *Summer Study Task Force on DoD Responses to Transnational Threats*, Vol. 1, *Final Report*, Washington, DC, 1997.

the overall nature of the terrorist threat to national security or national objectives. We have therefore tried to place terrorism and counterterrorism in strategic perspective (for example, how the terrorist instrument may relate to other forms of conflict, or its application as an "asymmetric strategy" by less-capable adversaries). In conceptualizing counterterrorism strategy, we have applied a strategic planning framework used successfully in other RAND studies outside the terrorism field.

Unlike many countries around the world, and unlike some of our allies, the United States has not faced an "existential" threat from terrorism, that is, a threat to our survival and basic way of life. The viability of the United States as a society and as a political system has not been, and very likely will not be, threatened by terrorist acts, however lethal. That said, terrorism affects our national interests directly and indirectly, and can constrain our international freedom of action. The potential for enormous increases in lethality and disruption as the result of unconventional terrorism reinforces the importance of counterterrorism as a part of our national security strategy. The stakes go beyond the protection of American lives and property and our capacity for global engagement, and involve the reasonable expectation that the government will keep its citizens from being terrorized.

The bulk of the research for this study was completed prior to the August 1998 bombings of the American embassies in Tanzania and Kenya, and the consequent U.S. strikes against terrorist-related targets in Afghanistan and Sudan, but reference has been made to them in the analysis where it seemed useful to do so.

STUDY APPROACH AND STRUCTURE

We build on a large body of previous RAND research on terrorism and political violence,[2] and make extensive use (especially in

---

[2]Some diverse and notable past RAND studies include: Brian Jenkins, *Future Trends in International Terrorism* (P-7176, 1985), *The Other World War* (R-3202-AF, 1985); *New Modes of Conflict* (R-3009-DNA, 1983), *The Likelihood of Nuclear Terrorism* (P-7119, 1985); Konrad Kellen, *On Terrorists and Terrorism* (N-1942-RC, 1982), *Terrorists—What Are They Like? How Some Terrorists Describe Their World and Actions* (N-1300-SL, 1979); and Bruce Hoffman, *Recent Trends and Future Prospects of*

Chapter Two on terrorism trends and future patterns) of the RAND-St. Andrews Chronology of International Terrorism, documenting incidents from 1968 to the present. The three papers in this volume were chosen because they give a good sense of the project and its key findings. Although the papers are broadly complementary, the reader will note some useful differences of perspective (most notably, the emphasis on terrorism's lethality in Chapter Two, and on its disruptive as well as destructive potential in Chapter Three). We have not attempted to eliminate these differences, which, in any case, serve as further contributions to informed debate.

Chapter Two, by Bruce Hoffman, charts trends and future patterns in international terrorism against civilian and military targets, and their implications. It also offers some broader observations on terrorist risks to the United States and the utility of military responses. The chapter describes the rise of new types of terrorists, changing motivations, and the traditionally incremental character of terrorists' tactical innovations (and suggests that most—but not all—terrorism will continue to follow this pattern). The author identifies the key factors behind the increasing lethality of international terrorist acts, despite a steady decrease in the overall number of incidents worldwide.

In Chapter Three, John Arquilla, David Ronfeldt, and Michele Zanini take up the controversial question of terrorism in the information age. They go beyond the discussion of "information warfare" by terrorists to assess the significance and organization of information-age terrorism and possible responses. Adopting a "netwar" perspective, they argue that future terrorism will often feature disruption rather than destruction, especially in a "war paradigm" where unconventional terrorism may be an attractive alternative to direct confrontation with the United States. Their chapter includes a revealing analysis of the information competence of terrorist organizations in the Middle East, and suggests that the more active and lethal of these make extensive use of information techniques and are increasingly organized as networks rather than hierarchies. The authors go on to

---

Terrorism in the United States (R-3618, May 1988), Recent Trends and Future Prospects of Iranian-Sponsored International Terrorism (R-3783-USDP, 1988), and "Holy Terror": The Implications of Terrorism Motivated by a Religious Imperative (P-7834, 1993). For an extensive list of RAND studies in this area, see RAND's Terrorism and Low-intensity Conflict bibliography (SB-1060).

propose ways in which the United States and the U.S. Air Force can equip themselves to address this modern form of terrorism, including opportunities for new information-intensive approaches to counterterrorism.

In the concluding chapter (Chapter Four), I seek to place terrorism and counterterrorism in strategic context, with special emphasis on the new dimensions of terrorism discussed in the previous chapters. I offer a typology of terrorist risks to U.S. interests, and discuss the changing geopolitics of terrorism. New regional and functional sources will compel us to look beyond the traditional centers of terrorism in Europe and the Middle East, and come to grips with terrorism as a transnational phenomenon, occupying an expanded place on the conflict spectrum. The discussion draws on the comparative experience of Israel, France, and Britain in addressing their own terrorism challenges. Finally, the chapter offers a framework for conceptualizing national counterterrorism strategy, with "core," "environment shaping," and "hedging" dimensions, and with special attention to the role of air and space power in relation to each.

Chapter Four's conclusions point to a strategy—and national capabilities—tailored to dealing with the very challenging problems of individuals, small nonstate actors, and networks in addition to the identifiable state sponsors that have been the traditional objects of air power in the service of counterterrorism. Counterterrorism strategy will be global, of necessity, but will also have to address the growing problem of homeland defense—a neglected dimension of American strategy.

Chapter Two

TERRORISM TRENDS AND PROSPECTS

Bruce Hoffman

INTRODUCTION

The bombings of the American embassies in Kenya and Tanzania in August 1998 demonstrate that terrorism is—and will remain—a central threat to international security as we approach the 21st century. Earlier events such as the June 1996 massive explosion outside a U.S. Air Force housing complex in Dhahran, Saudi Arabia, that killed 19 persons and wounded nearly 500 others, and the bombing the previous November of a joint Saudi-American military training center in Riyadh that killed four persons and wounded nearly 40, had already heightened concerns about terrorist targeting of U.S. military as well as diplomatic personnel and assets abroad.

This chapter examines facets of terrorism and likely prospects. We focus first on trends in international terrorism and, in particular, on the reasons behind terrorism's increasing lethality. We then consider the implications of these trends, with special reference to force protection and base security issues. Finally, we offer some concluding thoughts and an assessment of terrorism trends and patterns of activity.

TRENDS IN TERRORISM

Although the total volume of terrorist incidents worldwide has declined in the 1990s, the percentage of terrorist incidents resulting in fatalities has nonetheless grown. This section examines the reasons behind this trend and its implications for patterns of terrorist activity.

Terrorism's Changing Characteristics

In the past, terrorism was practiced by a collection of individuals belonging to an identifiable organization that had a clear command and control apparatus and a defined set of political, social, or economic objectives. Radical leftist (i.e., Marxist-Leninist/Maoist/ Stalinist movements) organizations such as the Japanese Red Army, the Red Army Faction in Germany, and the Red Brigades in Italy, as well as ethno-nationalist terrorist movements such as the Abu Nidal Organization, the Irish Republican Army (IRA), and the Basque separatist group, ETA, reflected this stereotype of the traditional terrorist group. They generally issued communiqués taking credit for—and explaining in great detail—their actions. However disagreeable or distasteful their aims and motivations may have been, their ideology and intentions were at least comprehensible—albeit politically radical and personally fanatical.

Significantly, however, these more familiar terrorist groups engaged in highly selective and mostly discriminate acts of violence. They targeted for bombing various symbolic targets representing the source of their animus (i.e., embassies, banks, national airline carriers, etc.) or kidnapped and assassinated specific persons whom they blamed for economic exploitation or political repression in order to attract attention to themselves and their causes. Even when these groups operated at the express behest of, or were directly controlled by, a foreign government, the connection was always palpable, if not necessarily proven beyond the shadow of legal doubt. For example, following the 1986 retaliatory U.S. air strike on Libya, Colonel Qaddafi commissioned the Japanese Red Army to carry out revenge attacks against American targets. In hopes of obscuring this connection, the Japanese group claimed its Libyan-sponsored operations in the name of a fictitious organization, that of the "Anti-Imperialist International Brigades."[1] Similarly, Iranian-backed terrorist opera-

---

[1] See Bruce Hoffman, *Inside Terrorism*, Columbia University Press, New York, 1998, pp. 188–189.

tions carried out by Hizbullah in Lebanon during the 1980s were perpetrated under the guise of the so-called "Islamic Jihad."[2]

Today, the more traditional and familiar types of ethnic/nationalist and separatist as well as ideological group have been joined by a variety of organizations with less-comprehensible nationalist or ideological motivations. These new terrorist organizations embrace far more amorphous religious and millenarian[3] aims and wrap themselves in less-cohesive organizational entities, with a more-diffuse structure and membership.[4] The bombings in Kenya and Tanzania evidence this pattern. Unlike the specific, intelligible demands of past familiar, predominantly secular, terrorist groups who generally claimed credit for and explained their violent acts,[5] no credible claim for the embassy attacks has yet been issued. Indeed, the only specific information that has come to light has been a vague message taking responsibility for the bombings in defense of the Muslim holy places in Mecca and Medina and promising to "pursue U.S. forces and strike at U.S. interests everywhere."[6]

Further, the embassy attacks themselves do not appear to have been undertaken by a specific existing or identifiable terrorist organization but instead are believed to have been financed by a millionaire Saudi Arabian dissident, Osama bin Laden, as part of his worldwide cam-

---

[2]See Magnus Ranstorp, *Hizb'allah in Lebanon: The Politics of the Western Hostage Crisis,* Macmillan, Houndmills, Basingstoke, and London, 1977, pp. 62–63, and U.S. Department of Defense, *Terrorist Group Profiles,* U.S. Government Printing Office, Washington, DC, 1988, p. 15.

[3]An example is the Aum Shinrikyo, the Japanese group responsible for the 1995 sarin nerve-gas attack on the Tokyo subway system.

[4]See, for example, the analysis in Neil King, Jr., "Moving Target: Fighting Terrorism Is Far More Perilous Than It Used to Be," *Wall Street Journal Europe,* August 25, 1998. See also the discussion below on the emergence of amateur terrorists as evidenced in the 1993 bombing of New York City's World Trade Center.

[5]Indeed, some groups—such as the Provisional Irish Republican Army—not only claimed responsibility for attacks but issued warnings in advance. The communiqués of various European left-wing terrorist groups have often been sufficiently voluminous to warrant their publication in collected volumes. See, for example, Yonah Alexander and Dennis Pluchinsky, *Europe's Red Terrorists: The Fighting Communist Organizations,* Frank Cass, London, 1992, *passim;* and Red Army Faction, *Texte der RAF (RAF Texts),* Verlag Bo Cavefors, Malmo, Sweden, 1977, *passim.*

[6]Quoted in Tim Weiner, "Bombings in East Africa: The Investigation; Reward Is Offered and Clues Studied in African Blasts," *New York Times,* August 11, 1998.

paign against the United States. In February 1998, for example, bin Laden supplemented his publicly declared war on the United States (because of its support for Israel and the presence of American military forces in Saudi Arabia) with a *fatwa*, or Islamic religious edict. With the issuance of this edict, bin Laden thereby endowed his calls for violence with an incontrovertible theological as well as political justification. To this end, he is believed to be able to call on the services of an estimated 4000–5000 well-trained fighters scattered throughout the Muslim world.[7] By comparison, many of the traditional, secular terrorist groups of the past were generally much smaller. According to the U.S. Department of Defense, for example, neither the Japanese Red Army nor the Red Army Faction ever numbered more than 20 to 30 hard-core members. The Red Brigades were hardly larger, with a total of fewer than 50 to 75 dedicated terrorists. Even the IRA and ETA could only call on the violent services of perhaps some 200–400 activists whereas the feared Abu Nidal Organization was limited to some 500 men-at-arms at any given time.[8]

The appearance of these different types of adversaries—in some instances with new motivations and different capabilities—accounts largely for terrorism's increased lethality in recent years. There are a number of implications for terrorism that perhaps portends for increased violence and bloodshed.

Terrorism's Increasing Lethality

Although the total volume of terrorist incidents worldwide has declined in the 1990s (see Figure 1), the percentage of terrorist incidents with fatalities has increased. According to the RAND-St. Andrews Chronology of International Terrorism,[9] a record 484

---

[7]Marie Colvin, Stephen Grey, Matthew Campbell, and Tony Allen-Mills, "Clinton gambles all on revenge," *Sunday Times*, London, August 23, 1998.

[8]U.S. Department of Defense, *Terrorist Group Profiles*, 1998, pp. 5, 35, 61, 64, 56, and 118.

[9]The RAND-St. Andrews Chronology of International Terrorism is a computerized database of international terrorist incidents that have occurred worldwide from 1968 to the present. The chronology has been continuously maintained since 1972 (when it was created by Brian Jenkins), first by RAND and since 1994 by the Centre for the Study of Terrorism and Political Violence at St. Andrews University, Scotland. The in-

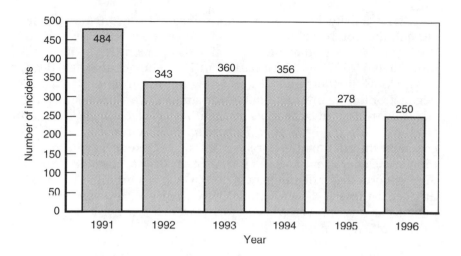

SOURCE: The RAND-St. Andrews Chronology of International Terrorism

Figure 1—Number of Worldwide Terrorist Incidents, 1991–1996

international terrorist incidents were recorded in 1991, the year of the Gulf War, followed by 343 incidents in 1992, 360 in 1993, 353 in 1994, falling to 278 incidents in 1995 and to only 250 in 1996 (the last calendar year for which complete statistics are available).[10] Indeed, the 1996 total was the lowest annual tally in 23 years. This overall

---

cidents in the chronology are concerned with *international terrorism,* defined here as incidents in which terrorists go abroad to strike their targets, select victims or targets that have connections with a foreign state (e.g., diplomats, foreign businessmen, offices of foreign corporations), or create international incidents by attacking airline passengers, personnel, or equipment. It excludes violence carried out by terrorists within their own country against their own nationals, and terrorism perpetrated by governments against their own citizens. *In this respect, it is emphasized that the data collected in the chronology comprise only a fraction of the total volume of terrorist violence, which in turn comprises a fraction of the violence of ongoing armed conflicts. Accordingly, the data contained in the chronology are not necessarily a definitive listing of every international and domestic terrorist incident that has occurred everywhere since 1968. Its value, accordingly, is as a means of identifying terrorist trends and projecting likely future terrorist patterns.*

[10]For the purposes of the RAND-St. Andrews Chronology of Terrorism, *terrorism* is defined by the nature of the act, not by the identity of the perpetrators or the nature of the cause. Terrorism is thus taken to mean violence, or the threat of violence, calculated to create an atmosphere of fear and alarm in the pursuit of political aims.

paucity of activity, however, was not reflected by a concomitant decline in the number of fatalities. On the contrary, 1996 was one of the bloodiest years on record. A total of 510 persons were killed: 223 more than in 1995 and 91 more than in 1994. In fact, the 1996 death toll ranks as the fourth highest recorded in the chronology since we began monitoring international terrorism in 1968. Significantly, the U.S. Department of State in its own authoritative compendium and analysis, *Patterns of Global Terrorism 1996*, cites a similar increase in international terrorism's lethality.[11] Hence, even though the State Department and the RAND-St. Andrews Chronology have different criteria for defining incidents (which, accordingly, produces different numerical tabulations),[12] we arrive at the same fundamental conclusion: even while terrorists were less active in 1996, they were significantly more lethal.

This development was mostly the result of a handful of so-called terrorist "spectaculars"—that is, the dramatic, attention-riveting, high-lethality acts that so effectively capture the attention of the media and public alike. Hence, although the number of international terrorist incidents that killed eight or more people increased only slightly in 1996 (from eight in 1995 to 13), the effect was nonetheless profound in that it was this relatively small number of incidents that accounted for the year's dramatically high body count.

International terrorism's overall trend toward increasing lethality is also reflected in the percentage of international terrorist incidents that result in one or more fatalities. For example, only 14 percent of all incidents in 1991 killed anyone, rising to 17.5 percent in 1992, 24 percent in 1993, and 27 percent in 1994 before reaching a record high of 29 percent in 1995. During 1996, admittedly, this percentage declined, as only 24 percent of incidents resulted in deaths. But at the

---

[11]Indeed, the second sentence of the first paragraph of the State Department report notes that "the total number of casualties [in 1996] was one of the highest ever recorded. . . ." Office of the Coordinator for Counterterrorism, *Patterns of Global Terrorism, 1996*, U.S. Department of State, Publication 10433, Washington, DC, April 1997, p. 1.

[12]The principal numerical differences between the RAND-St. Andrews Chronology's figures and the State Department's are in total number of international incidents (the State Department's figure is 296), number of fatalities (the State Department cites 311), and number of incidents with fatalities (the State Department notes 45 compared with the 60 that we identify).

same time, it should be recalled that even this smaller percentage is higher than the 17 percent average recorded during the 1970s and the 19 percent average during the 1980s.

A number of reasons account for terrorism's increased lethality. First, there appears to be a pattern that suggests that at least some terrorists have come to believe that attention is no longer as readily obtained as it once was. To their minds, both the public and media have become increasingly inured or desensitized to the continuing spiral of terrorist violence. Accordingly, these terrorists feel them-selves pushed to undertake ever more dramatic or destructively lethal deeds today in order to achieve the same effect that a less ambitious or bloody action may have had in the past. For example, when Timothy McVeigh, the convicted bomber of the Alfred P. Murrah Federal Building in Oklahoma City, was asked by his attorney whether he could not have achieved the same effect of drawing at-tention to his grievances against the U.S. government without killing anyone, he reportedly replied: "That would not have gotten the point across. We needed a body count to make our point."[13] In this respect, although the April 1995 bombing of the Murrah Building was doubtless planned well in advance, McVeigh may nonetheless have felt driven to surpass in terms of death and destruction the previous month's dramatic and more exotic nerve-gas attack on the Tokyo underground (perpetrated by the Japanese religious sect, the Aum Shinrikyo) to guarantee that his attack would be assured the requisite media coverage and public attention. This equation of publicity and carnage with attention and success thus has the effect of locking some terrorists onto an unrelenting upward spiral of violence to re-tain the media and public's interest.[14] Similarly, Ramzi Ahmad Yousef, the convicted mastermind of the 1993 New York City World Trade Center bombing, reportedly planned to follow that incident with the simultaneous in-flight bombings of 11 U.S. passenger airliners.[15]

---

[13]Quoted in James Brooke, "Newspaper Says McVeigh Described Role in Bombing," *New York Times*, March 1, 1997.

[14]See, for example, David Hearst, "Publicity key element of strategy," *The Guardian* (London), July 31, 1990; and David Pallister, "Provos seek to 'play havoc with British nerves and lifestyle'," *The Guardian* (London), July 31, 1990.

[15]James Bone and Alan Road, "Terror By Degree," *The Times Magazine* (London), October 18, 1997.

Second, terrorists have profited from past experience and have become more adept at killing. Not only are their weapons becoming smaller, more sophisticated, and deadlier,[16] but terrorists have greater access to these weapons through their alliances with various rogue states. During the 1980s, for example, Czechoslovakia reportedly sold 1000 tons of Semtex to Libya and an additional 40,000 tons to Syria, North Korea, Iran, and Iraq. All these countries, it should be noted, have long been cited by the U.S. Department of State as sponsors of international terrorism.[17]

Indeed, a third reason for terrorism's increased lethality, and one closely tied to the above point, is the active role played by states in supporting and sponsoring terrorism.[18] In its 1997 review of global terrorism patterns, the U.S. State Department designated seven countries as terrorism sponsors: Cuba, Iran, Iraq, Libya, North Korea, Sudan, and Syria. With the exception of the Sudan, which was added in 1993, each of these countries has remained on the list of terrorism patron-states for more than a decade.[19] The assistance that these governments has provided has often enhanced the striking power and capabilities of ordinary terrorist organizations, transforming some groups into entities more akin to elite commando units than the stereotypical Molotov-cocktail wielding or crude pipe-bomb manufacturing anarchist or radical leftist.[20]

---

[16]For example, the bomb used to destroy Pan Am 103 in 1988 is believed to have been a dual-timer/barometric pressure detonation device, constructed from less than 300 grams of Semtex plastic explosive, no bigger than the small radio it was concealed in. See "Explosive Detection Systems Boosted, Blasted at Hearing," *Counter-Terrorism and Security Intelligence,* February 12, 1990.

[17]On a state visit to Britain in 1990, Czech president Vaclav Havel observed that, "If you consider that 200 grams is enough to blow up an aircraft . . . this means world terrorism has enough Semtex to last 150 years." Quoted in Glenn Frankel, "Sale of Explosive to Libya Detailed," *Washington Post,* March 23, 1990.

[18]See Cindy C. Combs, *Terrorism in the Twenty-First Century,* Prentice Hall, Saddle River, New Jersey, 1997, pp. 86–88; Bruce Hoffman, *Recent Trends and Future Prospects of Iranian Sponsored International Terrorism,* RAND, R-3783-USDP, March 1990, *passim;* and Walter Laqueur, "Postmodern Terrorism," *Foreign Affairs,* Vol. 75, No. 5, September–October 1996, pp. 26–27.

[19]Office of the Coordinator for Counterterrorism, *Patterns of Global Terrorism,* 1996, p. 29.

[20]It is unlikely that an ordinary (e.g., nonstate-supported terrorist group) could have mounted the 1983 bombing of the U.S. Marine barracks at Beirut International Airport. In addition to the complex logistical and intelligence support that was pro-

State sponsorship has in fact a "force multiplying" effect on ordinary terrorist groups. It places greater resources in the hands of terrorists, thereby enhancing planning, intelligence, logistical capabilities, training, finances, and sophistication. Moreover, since state-sponsored terrorists do not depend on the local population for support, they need not be concerned about alienating popular opinion or provoking a public backlash.

The attraction for various renegade regimes to use terrorists as "surrogate warriors" has arguably increased since the 1991 Gulf War. The lesson of Iraq's *overt* invasion of Kuwait, where a UN-backed multinational coalition was almost immediately arrayed against Saddam, suggests that future aggressors may prefer to accomplish their objectives clandestinely with a handful of terrorist surrogates. Not only could such small bands facilitate the destabilization of neighboring or rival states, but if done covertly (and successfully), the state sponsor might escape identification, retaliation, and sanctions. Accordingly, terrorists may in the future come to be regarded by the globe's rogue states as an ultimate fifth column—a clandestine, cost-effective force used to wage war covertly against more powerful rivals or to subvert neighboring countries or hostile regimes.[21] Terrorism therefore could be employed as an adjunct to conventional warfare, and as a form of asymmetric strategy vis-à-vis the United States.

Fourth, the overall increase during the past 15 years of terrorism motivated by a religious imperative encapsulates the confluence of new adversaries, motivations, and tactics affecting terrorist patterns today (see Figure 2). While the connection between religion and ter-

---

vided to the terrorists, the weapon they used was not of the sort found in the typical terrorist group's arsenal. The truck bomb that destroyed the barracks and killed 241 Marines consisted of some 12,000 pounds of high explosives, whose destructive power was enhanced by canisters of flammable gases attached to the explosive device by its designers. The explosion was described at the time by FBI investigators as the "largest non-nuclear blast ever detonated on the face of the earth." Quoted in Eric Hammel, *The Root: The Marines in Beirut, August 1982–February 1984*, Harcourt Brace Jovanovich, San Diego, California, 1985, p. 303.

[21]Accusations of Iran's fomenting subversion in Bahrain and its alleged role in the bombing of the Khobar Towers military housing complex in Dhahran, Saudi Arabia, in July 1996 and of a joint Saudi-American military training facility in Riyadh in November 1995 may already be indicative of this trend.

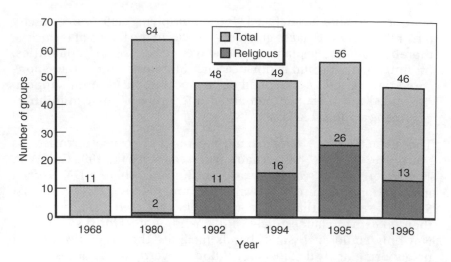

SOURCE: The RAND-St. Andrews Chronology of International Terrorism

Figure 2—Religious Versus Other Terrorist Groups

rorism is not new,[22] in recent decades this variant has largely been overshadowed by ethnic- and nationalist-separatist or ideologically motivated terrorism. Indeed, none of the 11 identifiable terrorist groups[23] active in 1968 (the year credited with marking the advent of modern, international terrorism) could be classified as religious.[24] Not until 1980 in fact—as a result of repercussions from the revolution in Iran the year before—do the first "modern" religious

---

[22]As David C. Rapoport points out in his seminal study of what he terms "holy terror," until the 19th century, "religion provided the only acceptable justifications for terror" (see David C. Rapoport, "Fear and Trembling: Terrorism in Three Religious Traditions," *American Political Science Review*, Vol. 78, No. 3, September 1984, p. 659).

[23]Numbers of active, *identifiable* terrorist groups from 1968 to the present are derived from the RAND-St. Andrews Chronology of International Terrorism.

[24]Admittedly, many contemporary terrorist groups—such as the overwhelmingly Catholic Provisional Irish Republic Army; their Protestant counterparts arrayed in various Loyalist paramilitary groups like the Ulster Freedom Fighters, the Ulster Volunteer Force, and the Red Hand Commandos; and the predominantly Muslim Palestine Liberation Organization—have a strong religious component by virtue of their membership. However, it is the political and not the religious aspect that is the dominant characteristic of these groups, as evidenced by the preeminence of their nationalist and/or irredentist aims.

terrorist groups appear,[25] although they amount to only two of the 64 groups active that year. Twelve years later, however, the number of religious terrorist groups has increased nearly six-fold, representing a quarter (11 of 48) of the terrorist organizations that carried out attacks in 1992. By 1994, a third (16) of the 49 identifiable terrorist groups could be classified as religious in character and/or motivation, and in 1995 they accounted for nearly half (26 or 46 percent) of the 56 known terrorist groups active that year. In 1996, however, only 13 (28 percent) of the 46 identifiable terrorist groups had a dominant religious component. Nevertheless, despite this decline in the 1996 figure, religion remained a significant force behind terrorism's rising lethality. Groups motivated in part or in whole by a salient religious or theological motivation committed ten of the 13 terrorist spectaculars recorded in 1996.[26]

The implications of terrorism motivated by a religious imperative for higher levels of lethality is evidenced by the violent record of various Shi'a Islamic groups during the 1980s. For example, although these organizations committed only 8 percent of all recorded international terrorist incidents between 1982 and 1989, they were nonetheless responsible for nearly 30 percent of the deaths during that time period.[27] Indeed, some of the most significant terrorist acts of recent years have had some religious element present. These include

- the 1993 bombing of New York City's World Trade Center by Islamic radicals who deliberately attempted to topple one of the twin towers onto the other;

- the series of 13 near-simultaneous car and truck bombings that shook Bombay, India, in February 1993, killing 400 persons and

---

[25]These are the Iranian-backed Shi'a groups *al-Dawa* and the Committee for Safeguarding the Islamic Revolution.

[26]The Palestinian Islamic Resistance Movement, Hamas, was responsible for three incidents (which killed a total of 56 persons); the Jammu and Kashmir Liberation Front for two (killing 37); a shadowy Saudi Arabian dissident group for two (causing 30 fatalities); the Egyptian al-Gama'a al-Islamiya for one (18 persons died); unspecified Kashmiri rebels for another incident (where eight persons died); and the Turkish Islamic Jihad for the remaining one (in which 17 persons perished).

[27]Between 1982 and 1989, Shi'a terrorist groups committed 247 terrorist incidents but were responsible for 1057 deaths.

injuring more than 1000 others, in reprisal for the destruction of an Islamic shrine in that country;

- the December 1994 hijacking of an Air France passenger jet by Islamic terrorists belonging to the Algerian Armed Islamic Group (GIA) and the attendant foiled plot to blow up themselves, the aircraft, and the 283 passengers on board precisely when the plane was over Paris, thus causing the flaming wreckage to plunge into the crowded city below;[28]

- the March 1995 sarin nerve-gas attack on the Tokyo subway system, perpetrated by an apocalyptic Japanese religious cult (Aum Shinrikyo) that killed a dozen persons and wounded 3796 others[29]; reportedly the group also planned to carry out identical attacks in the United States;[30]

- the bombing of an Oklahoma City federal office building in April 1995, where 168 persons perished, by two Christian Patriots seeking to foment a nationwide race revolution;[31]

- the wave of bombings unleashed in France by the Algerian GIA between July and October 1995, of metro trains, outdoor markets,

---

[28]The hijackers' plans were foiled after the French authorities learned of their intentions and ordered commandos to storm the aircraft after it had landed for refueling in Marseilles.

[29]Murray Sayle, "Martyrdom Complex," *The New Yorker*, May 13, 1996.

[30]Nicholas D. Kristof, "Japanese Cult Planned U.S. Attack," *International Herald Tribune* (Paris), 24 March 1997; and Robert Whymant, "Cult planned gas raids on America," *The Times* (London), March 29, 1997.

[31]It is mistaken to view either the American militia movement or other contemporary white supremacist organizations (from which McVeigh and his accomplice Terry L. Nichols came) as simply militant anti-federalist or extremist tax-resistance movements. The aims and motivations of these groups in fact span a broad spectrum of anti-federalist and seditious beliefs coupled with religious hatred and racial intolerance, masked by a transparent veneer of religious precepts. They are bound together by the ethos of the broader Christian Patriot movement that actively incorporates Christian scripture in support of their violent activities and use biblical liturgy to justify their paranoid call-to-arms. For a more detailed analysis, see Hoffman, *Inside Terrorism*, pp. 105–120. Further, it should be noted that McVeigh openly admitted to interviewers his belief in Christian Patriotism and involvement in Patriot activities, thus tacitly admitting his adherence to the theological belief system briefly described above. See Tim Kelsey, "The Oklahoma suspect awaits day of reckoning," *The Sunday Times* (London), April 21, 1996.

cafes, schools, and popular tourist spots, that killed eight persons and wounded more than 180 others;

- the assassination in November 1995 of Israeli Prime Minister Itzhak Rabin by a religious Jewish extremist and its attendant significance as the purported first step in a campaign of mass murder designed to disrupt the peace process;

- the Hamas suicide bombers who turned the tide of Israel's national elections with a string of bloody attacks that killed 60 persons between February and March 1996;

- the Egyptian Islamic militants who carried out a brutal machine-gun and hand-grenade attack on a group of Western tourists outside their Cairo hotel in April 1996 that killed 18;

- the June 1996 truck bombing of a U.S. Air Force barracks in Dhahran, Saudi Arabia, where 19 persons perished, by religious militants opposed to the reigning al-Saud regime;

- the unrelenting bloodletting by Islamic extremists in Algeria itself that has claimed the lives of more than an estimated 75,000 persons there since 1992;

- the massacre in November 1997 of 58 foreign tourists and four Egyptians by terrorists belonging to the Gamat al-Islamiya (Islamic Group) at the Temple of Queen Hatsheput in Luxor, Egypt; and

- the bombings of the U.S. embassies in Kenya and Tanzania in August 1998 that killed 257 and injured some 5000 others.

As the above incidents suggest, terrorism motivated in whole or in part by religious imperatives has often led to more intense acts (or attempts) of violence that have produced considerably higher levels of fatalities—at least compared with the relatively more discriminate and less lethal incidents of violence perpetrated by secular terrorist organizations. In brief, religious terrorism[32] tends to be more lethal than secular terrorism because of the radically different value sys-

---

[32]For a more complete and detailed discussion of this category of terrorist organization, see Bruce Hoffman, "Holy Terror: The Implications of Terrorism Motivated By a Religious Imperative," *Studies in Conflict and Terrorism*, Vol. 18, No. 4, Winter 1995, which was also published by RAND under the same title, P-7834, July 1993.

tems, mechanisms of legitimization and justification, concepts of morality, and Manichean world views that directly affect the "holy terrorists'" motivation.   For the religious terrorist, violence is a sacramental act or divine duty, executed in direct response to some theological demand or imperative and justified by scripture. Religion therefore functions as a legitimizing force, specifically sanctioning wide-scale violence against an almost open-ended category of opponents (i.e., all peoples who are not members of the religious terrorists' religion or cult). This explains why clerical sanction is so important for religious terrorists[33] and why religious figures are often required to "bless" (e.g., approve) terrorist operations before they are executed.

Fifth, the proliferation of amateurs taking part in terrorist acts has also contributed to terrorism's increasing lethality. In the past, terrorism was not just a matter of having the will and motivation to act, but of having the capability to do so—the requisite training, access to weaponry, and operational knowledge. These were not readily available capabilities and were generally acquired through training undertaken in camps run either by other terrorist organizations and/or in concert with the terrorists' state sponsors.[34]

Today, however, the means and methods of terrorism can be easily obtained at bookstores, from mail-order publishers, on CD-ROM, or over the Internet. Terrorism has become accessible to anyone with a grievance, an agenda, a purpose, or any idiosyncratic combination of the above. Relying on commercially obtainable bomb-making manuals and operational guidebooks, the amateur terrorist can be just as

---

[33]Examples are the aforementioned *fatwa* (Islamic religious edict) issued by bin Laden and the one issued by Iranian Shi'a clerics in 1989 calling for the novelist Salman Rushdie's death; the "blessing" given to the bombing of New York City's World Trade Center by the Egyptian Sunni cleric Sheikh Omar Abdel Rahman; the dispensation given by extremist rabbis to right-wing Jewish violence against Arabs in Israel, the West Bank, and Gaza; the approval given by Islamic clerics in Lebanon for Hizbullah operations and by their counterparts in the Gaza Strip for Hamas attacks; and the pivotal role over his followers played by Shoko Ashara, the religious leader of Japan's Aum Shinrikyo sect.

[34]Examples include the estimated dozen or so terrorist training camps long operated under Syria's aegis in Lebanon's Bekka Valley; the various training bases that have been identified over the years in the Yemen, Tunisia, the Sudan, Iran, Afghanistan, and elsewhere; and, of course, the facilities maintained during the Cold War by the Eastern Bloc.

deadly and destructive[35]—and even more difficult to track and antic-
ipate—than his professional counterpart.[36]

Amateur terrorists are dangerous in other ways as well. The absence
of a central command authority may result in fewer constraints on
the terrorists' operations and targets and—especially when combined with a religious fervor—fewer inhibitions about indiscriminate
casualties. Israeli authorities, for example, have noted this pattern
among terrorists belonging to the radical Palestinian Islamic Hamas
organization in contrast to their predecessors in the more secular,
professional, and centrally controlled mainstream Palestine Liberation Organization (PLO) terrorist groups. As one senior Israeli
security official noted of a particularly vicious band of Hamas terrorists: they "were a surprisingly unprofessional bunch . . . they had no
preliminary training and acted without specific instructions."[37]

In the United States, to cite another example of the lethal power of
amateur terrorists, it is suspected that the 1993 World Trade Center
bombers' intent was in fact to bring down one of the twin towers.[38]
By contrast, there is no evidence that the persons we once considered to be the world's arch-terrorists—Carlos, Abu Nidal, and Abu
Abbas—ever contemplated, much less attempted, destruction of a
high-rise office building packed with people.

---

[35]Examples of "amateurs" include the followers of Shoko Ashara who perpetrated the
Tokyo nerve-gas attacks; the two men who were convicted of mixing fertilizer and
diesel-fuel together to bomb the federal building in Oklahoma City; the Algerian
youths deliberately recruited into the terrorist campaign that was waged in Paris between July and October 1995 which had been initiated by their more professional
counterparts in the Armed Islamic Group (see the discussion immediately below); and
Israeli Prime Minister Rabin's assassin.

[36]Indeed, the situation that unfolded in France during this time period provides
perhaps the most compelling evidence of the increasing salience of amateurs recruited or suborned by professional terrorists for operational purposes. French authorities believe that, while professional terrorists belonging to the Algerian GIA may
have perpetrated the initial wave of bombings, like-minded amateurs—drawn from
within France's large and increasingly restive Algerian expatriate community—were
responsible for at least some of the subsequent attacks.

[37]Quoted in Joel Greenberg, "Israel Arrests 4 In Police Death," *New York Times*, 7 June
1993; and Eric Silver, "The Shin Bet's 'Winning' Battle," *The Jewish Journal* (Los
Angeles), June 11–17, 1993.

[38]Matthew L. Wald, "Figuring What It Would Take to Take Down a Tower," *New York
Times*, March 21, 1993.

Indeed, much as the "inept" World Trade Center bombers were derided for their inability to avoid arrest, their modus operandi arguably points to a pattern of future terrorist activities elsewhere. For example, as previously noted, terrorist groups were once recognizable as distinct organizational entities. The four convicted World Trade Center bombers shattered this stereotype. Instead they were like-minded individuals who shared a common religion, worshipped at the same religious institution, had the same friends and frustrations, and were linked by family ties as well, who simply gravitated toward one another for a specific, perhaps even one-time, operation.[39]

Moreover, since this more amorphous and perhaps even transitory type of group will lack the footprints or modus operandi of an actual, existing terrorist organization, it is likely to prove more difficult for law enforcement to build a useful picture of the dimensions of their intentions and capabilities. Indeed, as one New York City police officer only too presciently observed two months before the Trade Center attack: it was not the established terrorist groups—with known or suspected members and established operational patterns—that worried him, but the hitherto unknown "splinter groups," composed of new or marginal members from an older group, that suddenly surface out of nowhere to attack.[40]

Essentially part-time terrorists, such loose groups of individuals may be—as the World Trade Center bombers themselves appear to have been—indirectly influenced or remotely controlled by some foreign government or nongovernmental entity. The suspicious transfer of funds from banks in Iran and Germany to a joint account maintained

---

[39]The four bombers appear to have joined forces based on their attendance at the same place of worship (a Jersey City, New Jersey mosque). Family ties played a part as well: Ibrahim A. Elgabrowny, who although not charged with the Trade Center bombing specifically, was nonetheless implicated in the crime and was convicted in the subsequent plot to free the bombers, is the cousin of El Sayyid A. Nosair, who was implicated in the Trade Center bombing. Elgabrowny was among the 13 persons convicted in the follow-on plans to obtain the bombers' release, and was already serving a prison sentence in connection with the November 1990 assassination of Rabbi Meir Kahane. See Jim Mcgee and Rachel Stassen-Berger, "5th Suspect Arrested in Bombing," Washington Post, March 26, 1993; and Alison Mitchell, "Fingerprint Evidence Grows in World Trade Center Blast," New York Times, May 20, 1993.

[40]Interview with RAND research staff in New York City, November 1992.

by the accused bombers in New Jersey just before the Trade Center blast, for example, may be illustrative of an indirect or circuitous foreign connection.[41]   Moreover, the fact that two of the group's ringleaders—Ramzi Ahmed Yousef and Abdul Rahman Yasin—appear to have come to the United States specifically with the intent of orchestrating the attack raises suspicions that the incident may from the start have been planned and orchestrated from abroad.[42] Thus, in contrast to the Trade Center bombing's depiction in the press as a terrorist incident perpetrated by a group of amateurs acting either entirely on their own or as manipulated by Yousef, an individual portrayed by one of the bomber's defense attorneys as a "devious, evil . . . genius,"[43] the genesis of the Trade Center attack may be far more complex.

This use of amateur terrorists as dupes or cut-outs to mask the involvement of a foreign patron or government could potentially benefit terrorist state sponsors by enabling them to more effectively conceal their involvement and thus avoid potential military retaliation or diplomatic and economic sanctions. The prospective state sponsors' connection could be further obscured by the fact that much of the amateur terrorists' equipment, resources, and even funding could be entirely self-generating. The explosive device used at the World Trade Center, for example, was constructed out of ordinary, commercially available materials—including lawn fertilizer

---

[41]Federal authorities reported that they had traced nearly $100,000 in funds that had been wired to some of the suspects from abroad, including transfers made from Iran. An additional $8000 had been transferred from Germany into a joint bank account maintained by two of the bombers. Ralph Blumenthal, "$100,000 From Abroad Is Linked to Suspects in the Trade Center Explosion," New York Times, 15 February 1993. According to one of the other convicted bombers, Mahmud Abouhalima, funds had also been routed through the militant Egyptian Islamic group, Gamat al-Islamiya, whose spiritual leader is Sheikh Omar Abdel Rahman, who was convicted in connection with the June 1993 plot, and by the radical transnational Muslim Brotherhood organization. Additional financing reputedly was provided by and via Iranian businesses and Islamic institutions in Saudi Arabia and Europe. Mary B.W. Tabor, "Lingering Questions on Bombing," New York Times, September 14, 1994.

[42]Ralph Blumenthal, "Missing Bombing Case Figure Reported to Be Staying in Iraq," New York Times, June 10, 1993.

[43]Richard Bernstein, "Lawyer in Trade Center Blast Case Contends that Client Was a Dupe," New York Times, February 16, 1994. See also Tom Morganthau, "A Terrorist Plot Without a Story," Newsweek, February 28, 1994.

(urea nitrate) and diesel fuel—and cost less than $400 to build.[44] Indeed, despite the Trade Center bombers' almost comical ineptitude in avoiding capture (one member of the group attempted to collect the deposit for the demolished rental truck in which the bomb was concealed), they were still able to shake an entire city's—if not country's—complacency. Further, the simple bomb used by these amateurs proved just as deadly and destructive—killing six persons, injuring more than 1000 others, gouging out a 180-ft-wide crater six stories deep, and causing an estimated $550 million in damages to the twin tower and lost revenue to the business housed there[45]—as the more high-tech devices constructed out of military ordnance used by their professional counterparts.[46]

---

[44]The Trade Center bomb was composed of some 1200 lb of "common sulfuric and nitric acids used in dozens of household products and urea used to fertilize lawns." The detonating device was a more complex and extremely volatile mixture of nitro-glycerin enhanced by tanks of compressed hydrogen gases that were designed to increase the force of the blast. Richard Bernstein, "Lingering Questions on Bombing: Powerful Device, Simple Design," *New York Times*, September 14, 1994. See also Richard Bernstein, "Expert Can't Be Certain of Bomb Contents at Trial," *New York Times*, January 21, 1994. Richard Bernstein, "Nitro-glycerin and Shoe at Center of Blast Trial Testimony," *New York Times*, 27 January 1994; Richard Bernstein, "Witness Sums Up Bombing Evidence," *New York Times*, February 7, 1994; Edward Barnes et al., "The $400 Bomb," *Time*, March 22, 1993; and Tom Morganthau, "A Terrorist Plot Without a Story," *Newsweek*, February 28, 1994.

Similarly, in April 1988 a Japanese Red Army terrorist, Yu Kikumura, was arrested on the New Jersey Turnpike while en route to New York City on a bombing mission. Kikumura's mission was to carry out a bombing attack against a U.S. Navy recruiting station in lower Manhattan on 15 April to commemorate the second anniversary of the 1986 U.S. air strike against Libya. He is believed to have undertaken this operation at the behest of Libya's Colonel Qaddafi. Between his arrival in the United States on 14 March and his arrest a month later, Kikumura traveled some 7000 miles by car from New York to Chicago, through Kentucky, Tennessee, West Virginia, and Pennsylvania, purchasing materials for his bomb along the way. Found in his possession were gun-powder and hollowed-out fire extinguishers in which to place explosive materials and roofing nails to make crude anti-personnel weapons. Kikumura was sentenced to 30 years in prison. See Robert Hanley, "Suspected Japanese Terrorist Convicted in Bomb Case in New Jersey," *New York Times*, November 29, 1988; and Business Risks International, *Risk Assessment Weekly*, Vol. 5, No. 29, July 22, 1988.

[45]N. R. Kleinfeld, "Legacy of Tower Explosion: Security Improved, and Lost," *New York Times*, February 20, 1993; and Richard Bernstein, "Lingering Questions on Bombing: Powerful Device, Simple Design," *New York Times*, September 14, 1994.

[46]This is remarkably similar to the pattern of terrorist activity and operations that unfolded in France nearly two years later. See the discussion below.

Sixth, while on the one hand terrorism is attracting amateurs, on the other hand the sophistication and operational competence of the professional terrorists are increasing. These professionals are becoming demonstrably more adept in their tradecraft of death and destruction; more formidable in their capacity for tactical modification and innovation in their methods of attack; and more able to operate for sustained periods while avoiding detection, interception, or capture.

An almost Darwinian principle of natural selection thus seems to affect terrorist organizations, whereby every new terrorist generation learns from its predecessors—becoming smarter, tougher, and more difficult to capture or eliminate. Terrorists often analyze the mistakes made by former comrades who have been killed or apprehended. Press accounts, judicial indictments, courtroom testimony, and trial transcripts are meticulously culled for information on security force tactics and methods and then absorbed by surviving group members. The third generation of the now defunct Red Army Faction (RAF)[47] that emerged in the late 1980s is a classic example of this phenomenon. According to a senior German official, group members routinely studied court documents and transcripts of proceedings to gain insight into the measures employed by the authorities against terrorists. Having learned about these techniques—often from testimony presented by law enforcement personnel in open court (in some instances having been deliberately questioned on these matters by sympathetic attorneys)—the terrorists consequently are able to undertake the requisite countermeasures to avoid detection. For example, after learning that German police could obtain fingerprints from the bottom of toilet seats or the inside of refrigerators, surviving RAF members began to apply a special ointment to their fingers that, after drying, prevented fingerprints from being left and thus thwarted members' identification and incrimination.[48] As a spokesperson for the *Bundeskriminalamt* lamented in the months immediately preceding the RAF's unilateral declaration of a cease-

---

[47]The RAF's decision to disband (announced in April 1998) cited the group's growing political estrangement and isolation, rather than governmental countermeasures, as the most important reason for its dissolution.

[48]See Frederick Kempe, "Deadly Survivors: The Cold War Is Over But Leftist Terrorists In Germany Fight On," *Wall Street Journal*, December 27, 1991.

fire in April 1992, the "'Third Generation' learnt a lot from the mistakes of its predecessors—and about how the police works . . . they now know how to operate very carefully."[49] Indeed, according to a former member of the group, Peter-Juergen Brock (now serving a life sentence for murder), the RAF before the cease-fire had "reached maximum efficiency."[50]

Similar accolades have in recent years also been bestowed on the IRA. At the end of his tour of duty in 1992 as General Officer Commanding British Forces in Northern Ireland, General Sir John Wilsey described the organization as "an absolutely formidable enemy. The essential attributes of their leaders are better than ever before. Some of their operations are brilliant in terrorist terms."[51] By this time, too, even the IRA's once comparatively unsophisticated Loyalist terrorist counterparts had absorbed the lessons from their own past mistakes and had consciously emulated the IRA to become disquietingly more professional as well. One senior Royal Ulster Constabulary (RUC) officer noted this change in the Loyalists' capabilities, observing that they too were now increasingly "running their operations from small cells, on a need to know basis. They have cracked down on loose talk. They have learned how to destroy forensic evidence. And if you bring them in for questioning, they say nothing."[52]

In this respect, it is not difficult to recognize how the amateur terrorist may become increasingly attractive to either a more professional terrorist group and/or their state patron as a pawn or cut-out or simply as an expendable minion. In this manner, the amateur terrorist could be effectively used by others to conceal further the identity of the foreign government or terrorist group actually commissioning or ordering a particular attack. The series of terrorist attacks that unfolded in France conforms to this pattern. Between July and October 1995, a handful of terrorists using bombs fashioned with

---

[49]Quoted in Adrian Bridge, "German police search for Red Army Faction killers," *The Independent* (London), April 6, 1991.

[50]Quoted in Kempe, "Deadly Survivors."

[51]Quoted in Edward Gorman, "How to stop the IRA," *The Times* (London), January 11, 1992.

[52]Quoted in William E. Schmidt, "Protestant Gunmen Are Stepping Up the Violence in Northern Ireland," *New York Times*, October 29, 1991.

four-inch nails wrapped around camping-style cooking-gas canisters killed eight persons and wounded more than 180 others. Not until early October 1995 did any group claim credit for the bombings, when the radical GIA, a militant Algerian Islamic organization, took responsibility for the attacks. French authorities, however, believe that although professional terrorists perpetrated the initial bombings, like-minded amateurs—recruited by GIA operatives from within France's large and increasingly restive Algerian expatriate community—were responsible for at least some of the subsequent attacks.[53] Accordingly, these amateurs or new recruits facilitated the campaign's metastasizing beyond the small cell of professionals who ignited it, striking a responsive chord among disaffected Algerian youths in France and thereby increasing exponentially the aura of fear and, arguably, the terrorists' coercive power.

Finally, terrorism's increasing lethality may also be reflected in the fact that terrorists today tend to claim credit for their attacks less frequently. Unlike the more traditional terrorist groups of the 1970s and 1980s who not only issued communiqués explaining why they carried out an attack but proudly boasted of having executed a particularly destructive or lethal attack, terrorists are now appreciably more reticent. For example, some of the most serious terrorist incidents of the past decade, the so-called terrorist spectaculars, have never been credibly claimed—much less explained or justified as terrorist attacks—by the groups responsible. Events include

- the 1995 sarin nerve-gas attack on the Tokyo subway;

- the bombing of the Alfred P. Murrah Federal Office Building in Oklahoma City;

- the series of car bombings that convulsed Bombay in 1993, killing 317 persons; and

---

[53]For accounts of the bombing campaign, see, for example, Susan Bell, "16 hurt in Paris nail-bomb blast," *Times* (London), August 18, 1995; Adam Sage, "Paris faces autumn of terror as fifth bomb is discovered," *Times* (London), September 5, 1995; Adam Sage, "French hold 40 in hunt for bomb terrorists," *Times* (London), September 12, 1995; Alex Duval Smith, "Police fight 'war' in French suburbs," *Guardian* (London), November 1, 1995; and Craig R. Whitney, "French Police Arrest Suspected Leader of Islamic Militant Group," *New York Times*, November 3, 1995. See also "Terrorism: Political Backdrop to Paris Attacks," *Intelligence Newsletter* (Paris), No. 274, October 26, 1995, pp. 6–7.

- the huge truck bomb that destroyed a Jewish community center in Buenos Aires in 1994, killing 96.

The in-flight bombing of Pan Am 103, in which 278 persons perished, is an especially notorious example. Although we know that two Libyan government airline employees were identified and accused of placing the suitcase containing the bomb that eventually found its way onto the flight, no believable claim of responsibility has ever been issued.

The implication of this trend is that violence for some terrorist groups is perhaps becoming less a means to an end (that therefore has to be tailored and explained and justified to the public) than an end in itself that does not require any wider explanation or justification beyond the group's members themselves and perhaps their followers. Such a trait would conform not only to the motivations of religious terrorists (as previously discussed) but also to terrorist "spoilers"—e.g., groups bent on disrupting or sabotaging negotiations or the peaceful settlement of ethnic conflicts. That terrorists are less frequently claiming credit for their attacks may also suggest an inevitable loosening of constraints—self-imposed or otherwise—on their violence, which may in turn lead to higher levels of lethality.[54]

TERRORIST TACTICAL ADAPTATIONS ACROSS THE TECHNOLOGICAL SPECTRUM AND THEIR IMPLICATIONS

The trends described above shed light on a pattern of terrorist operations and tactical adaptation that underscores the dynamic and broad technological dimensions of the threat. These developments are likely to affect counterterrorism responses directly.

A key factor contributing to terrorism's rising lethality is the ease of terrorist adaptations across the technological spectrum. On the low

---

[54]For a more complete discussion of the no claim/increasing lethality issue, see Bruce Hoffman, "Why Terrorists Don't Claim Credit—An Editorial Comment," *Terrorism and Political Violence*, Vol. 9, No. 1, Spring 1997, and the more concise version published as "A New Kind of Terrorism: Silence is Deadlier," *Los Angeles Times* Sunday Opinion Section, August 18, 1996.

end of the technological spectrum, terrorists continue to rely on fertilizer bombs. These bombs' devastating effects have been demonstrated by the IRA at St. Mary Axe and Bishop's Gate in 1991 and 1992, at Canary Wharf and in Manchester in 1996, by the World Trade Center bombers, and by the men responsible for the Oklahoma City bombing. Fertilizer is perhaps the most cost-effective of weapons, costing on average 1 percent of a comparable amount of plastic explosive. To illustrate, the Bishop's Gate blast is estimated to have caused $1.5 billion[55] and the Baltic Exchange blast at St. Mary Axe $1.25 billion in damage.[56] The World Trade Center bomb cost only $400 to construct, but resulted in $550 million in damages and lost revenue to the business housed there.[57] Moreover, unlike plastic explosives and other military ordnance, fertilizer and at least two of its most common bomb-making counterparts—diesel fuel and icing sugar—are easily available commercially and completely legal to purchase and store, and are thus highly attractive "weapons components" for terrorists.[58]

On the high end of the conflict spectrum, one must contend with not only the efforts of groups like the apocalyptic Japanese religious sect, the Aum Shinrikyo, to develop nuclear in addition to chemical and

---

[55]William E. Schmidt, "One Dead, 40 Hurt as Blast Rips Central London," *New York Times*, April 25, 1993; and Richard W. Stevenson, "I.R.A. Says It Placed Fatal Bomb; London Markets Rush to Reopen," *New York Times*, April 26, 1993.

[56]William E. Schmidt, "One Dead, 40 Hurt as Blast Rips Central London," *New York Times*, April 25, 1993. See also William E. Schmidt, "With London Still in Bomb Shock, Major Appoints His New Cabinet," *New York Times*, April 12, 1992; "Delays Seen in London," *New York Times*, April 13, 1992; Peter Rodgers, "City bomb claims may reach £1bn," *The Independent* (London), April 14, 1992; and David Connett, "IRA city bomb was fertilizer," *The Independent* (London), May 28, 1992.

[57]Although, after adulteration, fertilizer is far less powerful than plastic explosive, it tends to cause more damage than plastic explosive because the energy of the blast is sustained and less controlled (see Roger Highfield, "Explosion could have wrecked city centre," *Daily Telegraph* (London), August 13, 1993). For example, the velocity of detonation of plastic explosive like Semtex occurs at about 8000 meters per second; the velocity of detonation of improvised explosives using ammonium nitrate (fertilizer) will typically occur at between 2000–3000 meters per second (depending on the mixture) and thus are less powerful (A. Bailey and S. G. Murray, *Explosives, Propellants and Pyrotechnics*, Brassey's, London, 1989, pp. 33–34; and Jimmie C. Oxley, "Non-Traditional Explosive: Potential Detection Problems," in Paul Wilkinson (ed.), *Technology and Terrorism*, Frank Cass, London, 1993, pp. 34–37.

[58]Roger Highfield, "Explosion could have wrecked city centre," *Daily Telegraph* (London), August 13, 1993.

biological capabilities,[59] but the proliferation of fissile materials from the former Soviet Union and the emergent illicit market in nuclear materials that is surfacing in Eastern and Central Europe.[60] Admittedly, although much of the material seen on sale as part of this black market cannot be classified as special nuclear material suitable for use in a fissionable explosive device, highly toxic radioactive agents can potentially be paired with conventional explosives and turned into a crude, nonfissionable radiological weapon. Such a device would not only physically destroy a target, but contaminate the surrounding area and render recovery efforts commensurably more difficult and complicated.[61]

Finally, at the middle range of the spectrum one sees a world awash in plastic explosives, hand-held precision-guided munitions (PGMs) that could be used against civilian and/or military aircraft, and automatic weapons that facilitate a wide array of terrorist operations.[62] In recent years, for example, surface-to-air missiles reputedly could be purchased on the international arms black market for

---

[59]For the most complete account of the Aum activities in this respect, see David E. Kaplan and Andrew Marshall, *The Cult at the End of the World: The Incredible Story of Aum*, Hutchinson, London, 1996, *passim*. See also John F. Sopko, "The Changing Proliferation Threat," *Foreign Policy*, No. 105, Winter 1996–97, pp. 12–14.

[60]See, for example, Graham T. Allison et al., *Avoiding Nuclear Anarchy: Containing the Threat of Loose Russian Nuclear Weapons and Fissile Material*, The MIT Press, Cambridge, Massachusetts, 1996; Frank Barnaby, "Nuclear Accidents Waiting To Happen," *The World Today* (London), Vol. 52, No. 4, April 1996; Thomas B. Cochran, Robert S. Norris, and Oleg A. Bukharin, *Making the Russian Bomb: From Stalin to Yeltsin*, Westview Press, Boulder, Colorado, 1995; William C. Potter, "Before the Deluge? Assessing the Threat of Nuclear Leakage from the Post-Soviet States," *Arms Control Today*, October 1995; Phil Williams and Paul N. Woessner, "Nuclear Material Trafficking: An Interim Assessment," *Transnational Organized Crime*, Vol. 1, No. 2, Summer 1995; and Paul N. Woessner, "Recent Developments: Chronology of Nuclear Smuggling Incidents, July 1991–May 1995," *Transnational Organized Crime*, Vol. 1, No. 2, Summer 1995.

[61]For example, a combination fertilizer truck bomb with radioactive agents would not only have destroyed one of the World Trade Towers, but rendered a considerable chunk of prime real estate in the world's financial nerve center indefinitely unusable because of radioactive contamination. The disruption to commerce that would be caused, the attendant publicity, and the enhanced coercive power of terrorists armed with such "dirty" bombs (which are arguably more credible threats than terrorist acquisition of fissile nuclear weapons) are fundamentally disquieting.

[62]See James Adams, *Engines of War: Merchants of Death and the New Arms Race*, Atlantic Monthly Press, New York, 1990, *passim*.

as little as $80,000.[63] Terrorists therefore now have relatively easy access to a range of sophisticated, off-the-shelf weapons technology that can be readily adapted to their operational needs.

The potential impact of cyberwar and information warfare on societies in general and on military facilities, communications, and operations in particular needs also to be considered. Terrorists or their state-patrons could attempt to sabotage networks in order to disrupt communications or even orchestrate disasters. Equally likely is terrorist targeting of classified (or other access-controlled) information systems to obtain intelligence with which to facilitate operations, or for counterintelligence purposes to more effectively thwart counterterrorism efforts. What is clear, however, is information warfare's potential force-multiplying effect on terrorist operations by providing such adversaries with either enhanced intelligence with which to facilitate more conventional terrorist operations or as a means to cause destruction and disruption without having to undertake actual physical attacks.[64]

Force Protection: The Example of IRA Targeting of British Forces in Northern Ireland

The Provisional Irish Republican Army's relentless quest to pierce the armor protecting the security forces in Northern Ireland illustrates the professional evolution and increasing operational sophistication of a terrorist group in affecting technological improvements and tactical adaptations. The first generation of early 1970s IRA de-

---

[63]See Steve LeVine, "U.S. now worries terrorists may get Stingers," *Washington Times*, December 31, 1991; Robert S. Greenberger, "Afghan Guerrilla Leader Armed by U.S., Hekmatyar, Could Prove Embarrassing," *Wall Street Journal*, May 11, 1992; and Richard S. Ehrlich, "For Sale in Afghanistan: U.S.-supplied Stingers," *Washington Times*, May 21, 1991.

[64]See John Arquilla and David Ronfeldt, "Cyberwar is Coming!" *Comparative Strategy*, Vol. 12, No. 2, pp. 141–165; Roger C. Molander, *Strategic Information Warfare: A New Face of War*, RAND, M-661-OSD, 1996; U.S. General Accounting Office, *Information Security: Computer Attacks at Department of Defense Pose Increasing Risks*, Washington, D.C., GAO/AIMD-96-84, May 1996; John Deutch, Director of U.S. Central Intelligence Agency, *Statement before the U.S. Senate Governmental Affairs Committee*, Permanent Subcommittee on Investigations, 25 June 1996; and U.S. Senate Permanent Subcommittee on Investigations (Minority Staff Statement), *Security in Cyberspace*, June 5, 1996.

vices, for example, were often little more than crude anti-personnel bombs, consisting of a handful of roofing nails wrapped around a lump of plastic explosive, that were detonated simply by lighting a fuse. Time bombs from the same era were hardly more sophisticated. They typically were constructed from a few sticks of dynamite and commercial detonators stolen from construction sites or rock quarries attached to ordinary battery-powered alarm clocks. Neither device was terribly reliable and often put the bomber at considerable risk. The process of placing and actually lighting the first type of device carried with it the inherent potential to attract attention while affording the bomber little time to effect the attack and make good his or her escape. Although the second type of device was designed to mitigate precisely this danger, its timing and detonation mechanism was often so crude that accidental or premature explosions were not infrequent, thus causing some terrorists inadvertently to kill themselves.[65]

In hopes of reducing these risks, the IRA's bomb makers invented a means of detonating bombs from a safe distance using model aircraft radio controls purchased at hobby shops. Scientists and engineers working in the British Ministry of Defence's (MoD) scientific research and development division in turn developed a system of electronic countermeasures and jamming techniques for the Army that effectively thwarted this means of attack.[66] However, rather than abandon the tactic completely, the IRA searched for a solution. In contrast to the state-of-the art laboratories, huge budgets, and academic credentials of their government counterparts, the IRA's own R&D department toiled in cellars beneath cross-border safe houses and in the back rooms of urban tenements for five years before devising a network of sophisticated electronic switches for their bombs that would ignore or bypass the Army's electronic countermeasures.[67]

---

[65]David Rose, "Devices reveal IRA know-how," *The Guardian* (London), May 18. 1990.

[66]Michael Smith, "IRA Use of Radar Guns in Bombings Described," *Daily Telegraph* (London), May 20, 1991.

[67]Smith, 1991. See also David Hearst, "IRA mines gap in army security," *The Guardian* (London), April 10, 1990; David Hearst, "'Human bomb' fails to explode," *The Guardian* (London), November 24, 1990; Jamie Dettmer and Edward Gorman, "Seven dead in IRA 'human' bomb attacks," *The Times* (London), October 25, 1990; and Will Bennett, "Terrorists keep changing tactics to elude security forces," *Independent* (London), December 17, 1991.

Once again, the MoD scientists returned to their laboratories, emerging with a new system of electronic scanners able to detect radio emissions the moment the radio is switched on—and, critically, just tens of seconds before the bomber can actually transmit the detonation signal. The very short window of time provided by this early warning of impending attack was just sufficient to allow Army technicians to neutralize the transmission signal and render detonation impossible.

For a time, this proved effective, but the IRA has discovered a means to overcome even this countermeasure. Using radar detectors, such as those used by motorists to evade speed traps, in 1991 the group's bomb makers fabricated a detonating system that can be triggered by the same type of hand-held radar gun used by police throughout the world to catch speeding motorists. Since the radar gun can be aimed at its target before being switched on, and the signal that it transmits is nearly instantaneous, the detection and jamming of such signals are extremely challenging.[68]

Finally, in the years before the 1994 IRA cease-fire, IRA units developed yet another means to detonate bombs using a photoflash "slave" unit that can be triggered from a distance of up to 800 meters by a flash of light. The device, which sells for between £60 and £70, is used by commercial photographers to produce simultaneous flashes during photo shoots. The IRA bombers can attach the unit to the detonating system on a bomb and activate it with a commercially available, ordinary flash gun.[69] The sophistication of this means of attack lies in its simplicity. Accordingly, those charged with defending against terrorism cannot discount the impact and consequences of even improvised weapons using relatively unsophisticated means of delivery, since the results can be equally as lethal and destructive.

---

[68]Bennett, 1991.

[69]Nicholas Watt, "IRA's 'Russian roulette' detonator," *The Times* (London), March 16, 1994; and, "Photoflash bomb threat to the public," *The Scotsman* (Edinburgh), March 16, 1994.

Implications for Antiterrorism and Force Protection

Although the technological mastery employed by the IRA may appear unique among terrorist organizations, experience has demonstrated repeatedly that, when confronted by new security measures, terrorists throughout the world will seek to identify and exploit new vulnerabilities, adjusting their means of attack accordingly.[70] This point is pertinent to the threat posed by terrorists to U.S. Air Force assets and personnel. The availability of a wide variety of weapons—from the most simple and basic to more sophisticated and technologically "cutting edge"—coupled with the terrorists' operational ingenuity has enabled at least some groups to stay ahead of the counterterrorist technology curve and repeatedly frustrate or defeat the security measures placed in their path. Relying on unconventional adaptations or modifications to conventional explosive devices, these organizations have been able to develop innovative and devastatingly effective means to conceal, deliver, and detonate all kinds of bombs.

An important lesson, therefore, is not to disregard an adversary's apparent lack of technological or operational sophistication and thereby be lulled into a false sense of security. In the context of terrorist attacks on Air Force assets, this has been demonstrated. In January 1981, a group of Puerto Rican terrorists penetrated the defenses surrounding the Muniz Air National Guard Base in Puerto Rico and, using simple explosive devices, destroyed eight A-7D fighters and one F-104 aircraft as well as damaging two other A-7Ds. Using relatively unsophisticated and comparatively inexpensive ordnance, they were able to inflict financial losses totaling more than $45 million.[71]

---

[70]As one high-ranking IRA terrorist explained, "You change your tactics to keep them guessing. It all depends on logistics. If you stick to one tactic, you can become predictable and be tracked down. They can find out when you work to a pattern." Quoted in Will Bennett, 1991.

[71]See Alan Vick, *Snakes in the Eagle's Nest: A History of Ground Attacks on Air Bases,* RAND, MR-553-AF, 1995, pp. 16, 154; and Bruce Hoffman, *Terrorism in the United States and the Potential Threat to Nuclear Facilities,* RAND, R-3351-DOE, January 1986, p. 9, and *Recent Trends and Future Prospects of Terrorism in the United States,* RAND, R-3618, May 1988, p. 42.

Moreover, even attacks that are not successful by conventional military measures can nonetheless still be a success for the terrorists provided that they are daring enough to garner media and public attention. Indeed, the terrorist group's fundamental organizational imperative to act—even if their action is not completely successful but brings them publicity—also drives their persistent search for new ways to overcome, circumvent, or defeat governmental security and countermeasures. Accordingly, attacks at all points along the conflict spectrum—from the crude and primitive to the most sophisticated—must be anticipated and appropriate measures employed to counter them.

CONCLUSION

Terrorists have targeted the United States more often than any other country.[72] This phenomenon is attributable as much to the geographical scope and diversity of America's overseas commercial interests and the large number of its military bases on foreign soil as to the United States' stature as the lone remaining superpower. Terrorists are attracted to American interests and citizens abroad precisely because of the plethora of readily available targets; the symbolic value inherent in any blow struck against perceived U.S. "expansionism," "imperialism," or "economic exploitation"; and, not least, because of the unparalleled opportunities for exposure and publicity from the world's most extensive news media that any attack on an American target assures. The reasons why the United States is so appealing a target to terrorists suggest no immediate reversal of this attraction. Indeed, the animus of many of the most radical Middle Eastern terrorist groups coupled with that of the principal state sponsors of international terrorism[73]—Iraq, Iran, Libya, Syria, North Korea, and the Sudan—suggests that the United States will remain a favored terrorist target. Accordingly, the U.S. Air Force, as an important vehicle of American overseas force projection and be-

---

[72]Followed by Israel, France, Great Britain, West Germany, the former Soviet Union/Russia, Turkey, Cuba, Spain, and Iran. The RAND-St. Andrews Chronology of International Terrorism.

[73]According to the U.S. Department of State's Office of the Coordinator for Counter-Terrorism. See U.S. Department of State, *Patterns of Global Terrorism, 1995*, Department of State Publication 10321, Washington, DC, April 1996, p. viii.

cause of the diverse range of targets it offers, will likely remain a focus of terrorist activity.

In terms of overall terrorism patterns and the future threat in general, the trends and developments examined here suggest three key conclusions.

First, we can expect little deviation from established patterns by mainstream terrorists belonging to traditional ethnic-separatist nationalist or ideologically motivated groups. They will largely continue to rely on the same two basic weapons that they have used successfully for more than a century: the gun and the bomb. Changes will occur in the realm of clever adaptations or modifications to existing off-the-shelf technology (as demonstrated by the IRA experience) or the continued utilization of readily available, commercially purchased materials that can be fabricated into crude—but lethally effective and damaging—weapons (such as the explosive devices used by the World Trade Center and Oklahoma City bombers, the IRA in its operations in England, and the bombers of U.S. embassies in Africa).

This adherence to a circumscribed set of tactics and limited arsenal of weapons will continue to be dictated by the operational conservatism inherent in the terrorists' organizational imperative to succeed. For this reason, traditional terrorists will always seek to remain just ahead of the counterterrorism technology curve: sufficiently adaptive to thwart or overcome the countermeasures placed in their path but commensurably modest in their goals (i.e., the amount of death and destruction inflicted) to ensure an operation's success. Traditional terrorist organizations will continue to be content to kill in the ones and twos and, at most, the tens and twenties, rather than embark on grandiose operations involving weapons of mass destruction (WMD) that carry with them the potential to kill on a much larger scale. Indeed, the pattern of definitively identified state-sponsored terrorist acts supports this argument. Despite the enhanced capabilities and additional resources brought to bear in these types of attacks through the assistance provided by radical governments and renegade regimes, without exception the terrorists' weapons have remained exclusively conventional (e.g., *not* involving chemical, biological, or nuclear agents) and have mostly conformed to long-established patterns of previous terrorist operations. In this respect, rather than attacking a particularly well-protected target set or attempting high-risk/potentially high-payoff operations, terrorists will merely search out and exploit hitherto unidentified vulnerabilities in their more traditional target sets and simply adjust their plan of attack and tactical preferences accordingly. This conclusion suggests that it will be difficult to deter terrorists completely, as any security hurdles placed in their path will not stop them from striking, but likely only displace the threat onto a softer target(s).

Second, the sophistication of terrorist weapons will continue to be in their simplicity. Unlike military ordnance, such as plastic explosives, for example, the materials used in homemade bombs are both readily and commercially available: thus, they are perfectly legal to possess until actually concocted or assembled into a bomb. These ordinary materials are difficult for authorities to trace or for experts to obtain a "signature" from. For example, the type of explosive used in the 1988 in-flight bombing of Pan Am flight 103 was Semtex-H, a plastic explosive manufactured only in Czechoslovakia and sold during the Cold War primarily to other former-Warsaw Pact countries as well as to such well-known state sponsors of terrorism as Libya, Iran, Iraq, Syria, and North Korea. In comparison, the materials used in the World Trade Center bomb, as previously noted, had no such foreign government pedigree, were entirely legal to possess, and could be traced only to an ordinary New Jersey chemical supply company. Hence, for foreign governments seeking to commission terrorist attacks or use terrorists as surrogate warriors, growing expertise in the fabrication of homemade materials into devastatingly lethal devices carries distinct advantages. Above all, it may enable the state sponsor to avoid identification and thereby escape military retaliation or international sanction. Terrorists, accordingly, will continue to use what they know will work. Most will not likely feel driven to experimentation with unconventional weapons, believing that they can achieve their objectives using readily available and/or conventional weapons.

Third, combinations of new types of terrorist entities with different motivations and greater access to WMD may surface to produce new and deadlier adversaries. Terrorism today increasingly reflects such a potentially lethal mixture: it is frequently perpetrated by amateurs; motivated by religious enmity, blind rage, or a mix of idiosyncratic motivations; and in some instances is deliberately exploited or manipulated by professional terrorists and their state sponsors. In this respect, the increasing availability of high-tech weapons from former-Warsaw Pact arsenals and the proliferation of fissile materials from the former Soviet Union and other Eastern Bloc countries[74] coupled with the relative ease with which some chemical or biological warfare agents can be manufactured, suggest that terrorists possessing these characteristics—particularly those with religious, millennialist, or apocalyptic motivations—would be most likely to cross into the WMD domain. Their trajectory along this path could be facilitated by any of the developments discussed in this volume that may already have made the means and methods of WMD more available on the world market.

Indeed, the post–Cold War order and the attendant possibilities and payoffs of independence, sovereignty, and power may also entice both new and would-be nations in addition to the perpetually disenfranchised to embrace terrorism as a solution to, or vehicle for, the realization of their aspirations. As such, there will be both ample motives and possibly abundant opportunities for terrorists that could portend an even bloodier and more destructive era of violence.

---

[74]Serious concerns have been raised about the evidently considerable security deficiencies and lax inventory and other control procedures that afflict the Russian nuclear archipelago—both military as well as civilian. It has been demonstrated that these once-lavishly funded facilities and their well-paid employees have languished in the post–Cold War era because of the often dire economic difficulties faced by Russia and the former-Soviet republics today. Accordingly, these same facilities are anemically funded, poorly managed, and beset with morale problems, creating the possibility of an illicit traffic in nuclear materials and accompanying black market in such goods that could be exploited or tapped into by terrorists, insurgents, revolutionaries, or other violent subnational entities.

Chapter Three

NETWORKS, NETWAR, AND INFORMATION-AGE TERRORISM

John Arquilla, David Ronfeldt, and Michele Zanini

The rise of network forms of organization is a key consequence of the ongoing information revolution. Business organizations are being newly energized by networking, and many professional militaries are experimenting with flatter forms of organization. In this chapter, we explore the impact of networks on terrorist capabilities, and consider how this development may be associated with a move away from emphasis on traditional, episodic efforts at coercion to a new view of terror as a form of protracted warfare. Seen in this light, the recent bombings of U.S. embassies in East Africa, along with the retaliatory American missile strikes, may prove to be the opening shots of a war between a leading state and a terror network. We consider both the likely context and the conduct of such a war, and offer some insights that might inform policies aimed at defending against and countering terrorism.

A NEW TERRORISM (WITH OLD ROOTS)

The age-old phenomenon of terrorism continues to appeal to its perpetrators for three principal reasons. First, it appeals as a weapon of the weak—a shadowy way to wage war by attacking asymmetrically to harm and try to defeat an ostensibly superior force. This has had particular appeal to ethno-nationalists, racist militias, religious fundamentalists, and other minorities who cannot match the military formations and firepower of their "oppressors"—the case, for example, with some radical Middle Eastern Islamist groups vis-à-vis Israel, and, until recently, the Provisional Irish Republican Army (PIRA) vis-à-vis Great Britain.

Second, terrorism has appealed as a way to assert identity and command attention—rather like proclaiming, "I bomb, therefore I am." Terrorism enables a perpetrator to publicize his identity, project it explosively, and touch the nerves of powerful distant leaders. This kind of attraction to violence transcends its instrumental utility. Mainstream revolutionary writings may view violence as a means of struggle, but terrorists often regard violence as an end in itself that generates identity or damages the enemy's identity.

Third, terrorism has sometimes appealed as a way to achieve a new future order by willfully wrecking the present. This is manifest in the religious fervor of some radical Islamists, but examples also lie among millenarian and apocalyptic groups, like Aum Shinrikyo in Japan, who aim to wreak havoc and rend a system asunder so that something new may emerge from the cracks. The substance of the future vision may be only vaguely defined, but its moral worth is clear and appealing to the terrorist.

In the first and second of these motivations or rationales, terrorism may involve retaliation and retribution for past wrongs, whereas the third is also about revelation and rebirth, the coming of a new age. The first is largely strategic; it has a practical tone, and the objectives may be limited and specific. In contrast, the third may engage a transcendental, unconstrained view of how to change the world through terrorism.

Such contrasts do not mean the three are necessarily at odds; blends often occur. Presumptions of weakness (the first rationale) and of willfulness (in the second and third) can lead to peculiar synergies. For example, Aum's members may have known it was weak in a conventional sense, but they believed that they had special knowledge, a unique leader, invincible willpower, and secret ways to strike out.

These classic motivations or rationales will endure in the information age. However, terrorism is not a fixed phenomenon; its perpetrators adapt it to suit their times and situations. What changes is the conduct of terrorism—the operational characteristics built around the motivations and rationales.

This chapter addresses, often in a deliberately speculative manner, changes in organization, doctrine, strategy, and technology that, taken together, speak to the emergence of a "new terrorism" attuned to the information age. Our principal hypotheses are as follows:

- **Organization.** Terrorists will continue moving from hierarchical toward information-age network designs. Within groups, "great man" leaderships will give way to flatter decentralized designs. More effort will go into building arrays of transnationally internetted groups than into building stand-alone groups.

- **Doctrine and strategy.** Terrorists will likely gain new capabilities for lethal acts. Some terrorist groups are likely to move to a "war paradigm" that focuses on attacking U.S. military forces and assets. But where terrorists suppose that "information operations" may be as useful as traditional commando-style operations for achieving their goals, systemic *disruption* may become as much an objective as target *destruction*. Difficulties in coping with the new terrorism will mount if terrorists move beyond isolated acts toward a new approach to doctrine and strategy that emphasizes campaigns based on swarming.

- **Technology.** Terrorists are likely to increasingly use advanced information technologies for offensive and defensive purposes, as well as to support their organizational structures. Despite widespread speculation about terrorists using cyberspace warfare techniques to take "the Net" down, they may often have stronger reasons for wanting to keep it up (e.g., to spread their message and communicate with one another).

In short, terrorism is evolving in a direction we call *netwar*. Thus, after briefly reviewing terrorist trends, we outline the concept of netwar and its relevance for understanding information-age terrorism. In particular, we elaborate on the above points about organization, doctrine, and strategy, and briefly discuss how recent developments in the nature and behavior of Middle Eastern terrorist groups can be interpreted as early signs of a move toward netwar-type terrorism.

Given the prospect of a netwar-oriented shift in which some terrorists pursue a war paradigm, we then focus on the implications such a development may have for the U.S. military. We use these insights to consider defensive antiterrorist measures, as well as proactive counterterrorist strategies. We propose that a key to coping with information-age terrorism will be the creation of interorganizational networks within the U.S. military and government, partly on the grounds that it takes networks to fight networks.

RECENT VIEWS ABOUT TERRORISM

Terrorism remains a distinct phenomenon while reflecting broader trends in irregular warfare. The latter has been on the rise around the world since before the end of the Cold War. Ethnic and religious conflicts, recently in evidence in areas of Africa, the Balkans, and the Caucasus, for awhile in Central America, and seemingly forever in the Middle East, attest to the brutality that increasingly attends this kind of warfare. These are not conflicts between regular, professional armed forces dedicated to warrior creeds and Geneva Conventions. Instead, even where regular forces play roles, these conflicts often revolve around the strategies and tactics of thuggish paramilitary gangs and local warlords. Some leaders may have some professional training; but the foot soldiers are often people who, for one reason or another, get caught in a fray and learn on the job. Adolescents and children with high-powered weaponry are taking part in growing numbers. In many of these conflicts, savage acts are increasingly committed without anyone taking credit—it may not even be clear which side is responsible. The press releases of the protagonists sound high-minded and self-legitimizing, but the reality at the local level is often about clan rivalries and criminal ventures (e.g., looting, smuggling, or protection rackets).[1]

Thus, irregular warfare has become endemic and vicious around the world. A decade or so ago, terrorism was a rather distinct entry on the spectrum of conflict, with its own unique attributes. Today, it seems increasingly connected with these broader trends in irregular warfare, especially as waged by nonstate actors. As Martin Van Creveld warns:

> In today's world, the main threat to many states, including specifi-
> cally the U.S., no longer comes from other states. Instead, it comes
> from small groups and other organizations which are not states.

---

[1]For an illuminating take on irregular warfare that emphasizes the challenges to the Red Cross, see Michael Ignatieff, "Unarmed Warriors," *The New Yorker*, March 24, 1997, pp. 56–71.

Either we make the necessary changes and face them today, or what is commonly known as the modern world will lose all sense of security and will dwell in perpetual fear.[2]

Meanwhile, for the past several years, terrorism experts have broadly concurred that this phenomenon will persist, if not get worse. General agreement that terrorism may worsen parses into different scenarios. For example, Walter Laqueur warns that religious motivations could lead to "superviolence," with millenarian visions of a coming apocalypse driving "postmodern" terrorism. Fred Iklé worries that increased violence may be used by terrorists to usher in a new totalitarian age based on Leninist ideals. Bruce Hoffman raises the prospect that religiously-motivated terrorists may escalate their violence in order to wreak sufficient havoc to undermine the world political system and replace it with a chaos that is particularly detrimental to the United States—a basically nihilist strategy.[3]

The preponderance of U.S. conventional power may continue to motivate some state and nonstate adversaries to opt for terror as an asymmetric response. Technological advances and underground trafficking may make weapons of mass destruction (WMD—nuclear, chemical, biological weapons) ever easier for terrorists to acquire.[4] Terrorists' shifts toward looser, less hierarchical organizational structures, and their growing use of advanced communications technologies for command, control, and coordination, may further empower small terrorist groups and individuals who want to mount operations from a distance.

There is also agreement about an emergence of two tiers of terror: one characterized by hard-core professionals, the other by amateur

---

[2]Martin Van Creveld, "In Wake of Terrorism, Modern Armies Prove to Be Dinosaurs of Defense," *New Perspectives Quarterly,* Vol. 13, No. 4, Fall 1996, p. 58.

[3]See Walter Laqueur, "Postmodern Terrorism," *Foreign Affairs,* Vol. 75, No. 5, September/October 1996, pp. 24–36; Fred Iklé, "The Problem of the Next Lenin," *The National Interest,* Vol. 47, Spring 1997, pp. 9–19; Bruce Hoffman, *Responding to Terrorism Across the Technological Spectrum,* RAND, P-7874, 1994; Bruce Hoffman, *Inside Terrorism,* Columbia University Press, New York, 1998; Robert Kaplan, "The Coming Anarchy," *Atlantic Monthly,* February 1994, pp. 44–76.

[4]See J. Kenneth Campbell, "Weapon of Mass Destruction Terrorism," Master's thesis, Naval Postgraduate School, Monterey, California, 1996.

cut-outs.[5] The deniability gained by terrorists operating through willing amateurs, coupled with the increasing accessibility of ever more destructive weaponry, has also led many experts to concur that terrorists will be attracted to engaging in more lethal destruction, with increased targeting of information and communications infrastructures.[6]

Some specialists also suggest that "information" will become a key target—both the conduits of information infrastructures and the content of information, particularly the media.[7] While these target-sets may involve little lethal activity, they offer additional theaters of operations for terrorists. Laqueur in particular foresees that, "If the new terrorism directs its energies toward information warfare, its destructive power will be exponentially greater than any it wielded in the past—greater even than it would be with biological and chemical weapons."[8] New planning and scenario-building is needed to help think through how to defend against this form of terrorism.[9]

Such dire predictions have galvanized a variety of responses, which range from urging the creation of international control regimes over the tools of terror (such as WMD materials and advanced encryption capabilities), to the use of coercive diplomacy against state sponsors of terror. Increasingly, the liberal use of military force against terrorists has also been recommended. Caleb Carr in particular espoused this theme, sparking a heated debate.[10] Today, many leading works

---

[5]Bruce Hoffman and Caleb Carr, "Terrorism: Who Is Fighting Whom?" *World Policy Journal*, Vol. 14, No. 1, Spring 1997, pp. 97–104.

[6]For instance, Martin Shubik, "Terrorism, Technology, and the Socioeconomics of Death," *Comparative Strategy*, Vol. 16, No. 4, October–December 1997, pp. 399–414; as well as Hoffman, 1998.

[7]See Matthew Littleton, "Information Age Terrorism," MA thesis, U.S. Naval Postgraduate School, 1995, and Brigitte Nacos, *Terrorism and the Media*, Columbia University Press, New York, 1994.

[8]Laqueur, 1996, p. 35.

[9]For more on this issue, see Roger Molander, Andrew Riddile, and Peter Wilson, *Strategic Information Warfare: A New Face of War*, RAND, MR-661-OSD, 1996; Roger Molander, Peter Wilson, David Mussington, and Richard Mesic, *Strategic Information Warfare Rising*, RAND, 1998.

[10]Caleb Carr, "Terrorism as Warfare," *World Policy Journal*, Vol. 13, No. 4, Winter 1996–1997, pp. 1–12. This theme was advocated early by Gayle Rivers, *The War*

on combating terrorism blend notions of control mechanisms, international regimes, and the use of force.[11]

Against this background, experts have begun to recognize the growing role of networks—of networked organizational designs and related doctrines, strategies, and technologies—among the practitioners of terrorism. The growth of these networks is related to the spread of advanced information technologies that allow dispersed groups, and individuals, to conspire and coordinate across considerable distances. Recent U.S. efforts to investigate and attack the bin Laden network (named for the central influence of Osama bin Laden) attest to this. The rise of networks is likely to reshape terrorism in the information age, and lead to the adoption of netwar—a kind of information-age conflict that will be waged principally by nonstate actors. Our contribution to this volume is to present the concept of netwar and show how terrorism is being affected by it.

THE ADVENT OF NETWAR—ANALYTICAL BACKGROUND[12]

The information revolution is altering the nature of conflict across the spectrum. Of the many reasons for this, we call attention to two in particular. First, the information revolution is favoring and strengthening network forms of organization, often giving them an advantage over hierarchical forms. The rise of networks means that power is migrating to nonstate actors, who are able to organize into sprawling multi-organizational networks (especially all-channel networks, in which every node is connected to every other node) more readily than can traditional, hierarchical, state actors. Nonstate-actor networks are thought to be more flexible and responsive than hierarchies in reacting to outside developments, and

---

Against the Terrorists: How to Fight and Win, Stein and Day, New York, 1986. For more on the debate, see Hoffman and Carr, 1997.

[11]See, for instance, Benjamin Netanyahu, *Winning the War Against Terrorism,* Simon and Schuster, New York, 1996, and John Kerry (Senator), *The New War,* Simon & Schuster, New York, 1997.

[12]This analytical background is drawn from John Arquilla and David Ronfeldt, *The Advent of Netwar,* RAND, MR-678-OSD, 1996, and David Ronfeldt, John Arquilla, Graham Fuller, and Melissa Fuller, *The Zapatista "Social Netwar" in Mexico,* RAND, MR-994-A, forthcoming. Also see John Arquilla and David Ronfeldt (eds.), *In Athena's Camp: Preparing for Conflict in the Information Age,* RAND, MR-880-OSD/RC, 1997.

to be better than hierarchies at using information to improve deci-sionmaking.[13]

Second, as the information revolution deepens, conflicts will increas-ingly depend on information and communications matters. More than ever before, conflicts will revolve around "knowledge" and the use of "soft power."[14] Adversaries will emphasize "information op-erations" and "perception management"—that is, media-oriented measures that aim to attract rather than coerce, and that affect how secure a society, a military, or other actor feels about its knowledge of itself and of its adversaries. Psychological disruption may become as important a goal as physical destruction.

Thus, major transformations are coming in the nature of adversaries, in the type of threats they may pose, and in how conflicts can be waged. Information-age threats are likely to be more diffuse, dis-persed, multidimensional, and ambiguous than more traditional threats. Metaphorically, future conflicts may resemble the Oriental game of *Go* more than the Western game of chess. The conflict spec-trum will be molded from end to end by these dynamics:

- *Cyberwar*—a concept that refers to information-oriented military warfare—is becoming an important entry at the military end of the spectrum, where the language has normally been about high-intensity conflicts (HICs).

- *Netwar* figures increasingly at the societal end of the spectrum, where the language has normally been about low-intensity con-flict (LIC), operations other than war (OOTW), and nonmilitary modes of conflict and crime. [15]

---

[13]For background on this issue, see Charles Heckscher, "Defining the Post-Bureaucratic Type," in Charles Heckscher and Anne Donnelon (eds.), *The Post-Bureaucratic Organization*, Sage, Thousand Oaks, California, 1995, pp. 50–52.

[14]The concept of soft power was introduced by Joseph S. Nye in *Bound to Lead: The Changing Nature of American Power*, Basic Books, New York, 1990, and further elaborated in Joseph S. Nye, and William A. Owens, "America's Information Edge," *Foreign Affairs*, Vol. 75, No. 2, March/April 1996.

[15]For more on information-age conflict, netwar, and cyberwar, see John Arquilla and David Ronfeldt, "Cyberwar is Coming!" *Comparative Strategy*, Vol. 12, No. 2, Summer 1993, pp. 141–165, and Arquilla and Ronfeldt, 1996 and 1997.

Whereas cyberwar usually pits formal military forces against each other, netwar is more likely to involve nonstate, paramilitary, and irregular forces—as in the case of terrorism. Both concepts are consistent with the views of analysts such as Van Creveld, who believe that a "transformation of war" is under way.[16] Neither concept is just about technology; both refer to *comprehensive* approaches to conflict—comprehensive in that they mix organizational, doctrinal, strategic, tactical, and technological innovations, for offense and defense.

Definition of Netwar

To be more precise, *netwar* refers to an emerging mode of conflict and crime at societal levels, involving measures short of traditional war, in which the protagonists use network forms of organization and related doctrines, strategies, and technologies attuned to the information age. These protagonists are likely to consist of dispersed small groups who communicate, coordinate, and conduct their campaigns in an internetted manner, without a precise central command. Thus, information-age netwar differs from modes of conflict and crime in which the protagonists prefer formal, stand-alone, hierarchical organizations, doctrines, and strategies, as in past efforts, for example, to build centralized movements along Marxist lines.

The term is meant to call attention to the prospect that network-based conflict and crime will become major phenomena in the decades ahead. Various actors across the spectrum of conflict and crime are already evolving in this direction. To give a string of examples, netwar is about the Middle East's Hamas more than the Palestine Liberation Organization (PLO), Mexico's Zapatistas more than Cuba's Fidelistas, and the American Christian Patriot movement more than the Ku Klux Klan. It is also about the Asian Triads more than the Sicilian Mafia, and Chicago's Gangsta Disciples more than the Al Capone Gang.

This spectrum includes familiar adversaries who are modifying their structures and strategies to take advantage of networked designs,

---

[16]Martin Van Creveld, *The Transformation of War*, Free Press, New York, 1991.

such as transnational terrorist groups, black-market proliferators of WMD, transnational crime syndicates, fundamentalist and ethno-nationalist movements, intellectual property and high-sea pirates, and smugglers of black-market goods or migrants. Some urban gangs, back-country militias, and militant single-issue groups in the United States are also developing netwar-like attributes. In addition, there is a new generation of radicals and activists who are just beginning to create information-age ideologies, in which identities and loyalties may shift from the nation-state to the transnational level of global civil society. New kinds of actors, such as anarchistic and nihilistic leagues of computer-hacking "cyboteurs," may also partake of netwar.

Many—if not most—netwar actors will be nonstate. Some may be agents of a state, but others may try to turn states into *their* agents. Moreover, a netwar actor may be both subnational and transnational in scope. Odd hybrids and symbioses are likely. Furthermore, some actors (e.g., violent terrorist and criminal organizations) may threaten U.S. and other nations' interests, but other netwar actors (e.g., peaceful social activists) may not. Some may aim at destruction, others at disruption. Again, many variations are possible.

The full spectrum of netwar proponents may thus seem broad and odd at first glance. But there is an underlying pattern that cuts across all variations: *the use of network forms of organization, doctrine, strategy, and technology attuned to the information age.*

More About Organizational Design

The notion of an organizational structure qualitatively different from traditional hierarchical designs is not recent; for example, in the early 1960s Burns and Stalker referred to the *organic* form as "a network structure of control, authority, and communication," with "lateral rather than vertical direction of communication." In organic structure,[17]

---

[17]T. Burns and G. M. Stalker, *The Management of Innovation*, Tavistock, London, 1961, p. 121.

omniscience [is] no longer imputed to the head of the concern; knowledge about the technical or commercial nature of the here and now task may be located anywhere in the network; [with] this location becoming the ad hoc centre of control authority and communication.

In the business world, virtual or networked organizations are being heralded as effective alternatives to bureaucracies—as in the case of Eastman Chemical Company and the Shell-Sarnia Plant—because of their inherent flexibility, adaptiveness, and ability to capitalize on the talents of all members of the organization.[18]

What has long been emerging in the business world is now becoming apparent in the organizational structures of netwar actors. In an archetypal netwar, the protagonists are likely to amount to a set of diverse, dispersed "nodes" who share a set of ideas and interests and who are arrayed to act in a fully internetted "all-channel" manner. Networks come in basically three types (or topologies) (see Figure 3):[19]

- The *chain* network, as in a smuggling chain where people, goods, or information move along a line of separated contacts, and where end-to-end communication must travel through the intermediate nodes.

- The *star*, hub, or wheel network, as in a franchise or a cartel structure where a set of actors is tied to a central node or actor, and must go through that node to communicate and coordinate.

- The *all-channel* network, as in a collaborative network of militant small groups where every group is connected to every other.

Each node in the diagrams of Figure 3 may be to an individual, a group, an institution, part of a group or institution, or even a state. The nodes may be large or small, tightly or loosely coupled, and in-

---

[18]See, for instance, Jessica Lipnack and Jeffrey Stamps, *The Age of the Network*, Wiley & Sons, New York, 1994, pp. 51–78, and Heckscher, "Defining the Post-Bureaucratic Type," p. 45.

[19]Adapted from William M. Evan, "An Organization-Set Model of Interorganizational Relations," in Matthew Tuite, Roger Chisholm, and Michael Radnor (eds.), *Interorganizational Decisionmaking*, Aldine Publishing Company, Chicago, 1972.

clusive or exclusive in membership. They may be segmentary or specialized—that is, they may look alike and engage in similar activities, or they may undertake a division of labor based on specialization. The boundaries of the network may be well defined, or blurred and porous in relation to the outside environment. All such variations are possible.

Each type may be suited to different conditions and purposes, and all three may be found among netwar-related adversaries—e.g., the chain in smuggling operations, the star at the core of terrorist and criminal syndicates, and the all-channel type among militant groups that are highly internetted and decentralized. There may also be hybrids. For example, a netwar actor may have an all-channel council at its core, but use stars and chains for tactical operations. There may also be hybrids of network and hierarchical forms of organization, and hierarchies may exist inside particular nodes in a network. Some actors may have a hierarchical organization overall, but use networks for tactical operations; other actors may have an all-channel network design, but use hierarchical teams for tactical operations. Again, many configurations are possible, and it may be difficult for an analyst to discern exactly what type of networking characterizes a particular actor.

Of the three network types, the all-channel has been the most difficult to organize and sustain historically, partly because it may require dense communications. However, it gives the network form the most potential for collaborative undertakings, and it is the type

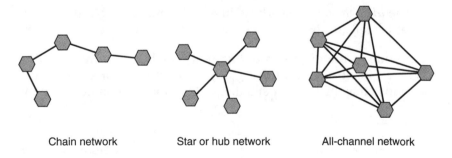

Chain network   Star or hub network   All-channel network

Figure 3—Types of Networks

that is gaining strength from the information revolution. Pictorially, an all-channel netwar actor resembles a geodesic "Bucky ball" (named for Buckminster Fuller); it does not resemble a pyramid. The design is flat. Ideally, there is no single, central leadership, command, or headquarters—no precise heart or head that can be targeted. The network as a whole (but not necessarily each node) has little to no hierarchy, and there may be multiple leaders. Decision-making and operations are decentralized, allowing for local initiative and autonomy. Thus the design may sometimes appear acephalous (headless), and at other times polycephalous (Hydra-headed).[20]

The capacity of this design for effective performance over time may depend on the presence of shared principles, interests, and goals—at best, an overarching doctrine or ideology—that spans all nodes and to which the members wholeheartedly subscribe. Such a set of principles, shaped through mutual consultation and consensus-building, can enable them to be "all of one mind," even though they are dispersed and devoted to different tasks. It can provide a central ideational, strategic, and operational coherence that allows for tactical decentralization. It can set boundaries and provide guidelines for decisions and actions so that the members do not have to resort to a hierarchy—"they know what they have to do."[21]

The network design may depend on having an infrastructure for the dense communication of functional information. All nodes are not necessarily in constant communication, which may not make sense for a secretive, conspiratorial actor. But when communication is needed, the network's members must be able to disseminate information promptly and as broadly as desired within the network and to outside audiences.

---

[20]The structure may also be cellular, although the presence of cells does not necessarily mean a network exists. A hierarchy can also be cellular, as is the case with some subversive organizations. A key difference between cells and nodes is that the former are designed to minimize information flows for security reasons (usually only the head of the cell reports to the leadership), while nodes in principle can easily establish connections with other parts of the network (so that communications and coordination can occur horizontally).

[21]The quotation is from a doctrinal statement by Louis Beam about "leaderless resistance," which has strongly influenced right-wing white-power groups in the United States. See The Seditionist, Issue 12, February 1992.

In many respects, then, the archetypal netwar design corresponds to what earlier analysts called a "segmented, polycentric, ideologically integrated network" (SPIN):[22]

> By segmentary I mean that it is cellular, composed of many different groups. . . . By polycentric I mean that it has many different leaders or centers of direction. . . . By networked I mean that the segments and the leaders are integrated into reticulated systems or networks through various structural, personal, and ideological ties. Networks are usually unbounded and expanding. . . . This acronym [SPIN] helps us picture this organization as a fluid, dynamic, expanding one, spinning out into mainstream society.

Caveats About the Role of Technology

To realize its potential, a fully interconnected network requires a capacity for constant, dense information and communications flows, more so than do other forms of organization (e.g., hierarchies). This capacity is afforded by the latest information and communications technologies—cellular telephones, fax machines, electronic mail (e-mail), World Wide Web (WWW) sites, and computer conferencing. Moreover, netwar agents are poised to benefit from future increases in the speed of communication, dramatic reductions in the costs of communication, increases in bandwidth, vastly expanded connectivity, and integration of communication with computing technologies.[23] Such technologies are highly advantageous for a netwar actor whose constituents are geographically dispersed.

---

[22]See Luther P. Gerlach, "Protest Movements and the Construction of Risk," in B. B. Johnson and V. T. Covello (eds.), *The Social and Cultural Construction of Risk*, D. Reidel Publishing Co., Boston, Massachusetts, 1987, p. 115, based on Luther P. Gerlach and Virginia Hine, *People, Power, Change: Movements of Social Transformation*, The Bobbs-Merrill Co., New York, 1970. This SPIN concept, a precursor of the netwar concept, was proposed by Luther Gerlach and Virginia Hine in the 1960s to depict U.S. social movements. It anticipates many points about network forms of organization that are now coming into focus in the analysis not only of social movements but also some terrorist, criminal, ethno-nationalist, and fundamentalist organizations.

[23]See Wolf V. Heydenbrand, "New Organizational Forms," *Work and Occupations*, No. 3, Vol. 16, August 1989, pp. 323–357.

However, caveats are in order. First, the new technologies, however enabling for organizational networking, may not be the only crucial technologies for a netwar actor. Old means of communications such as human couriers, and mixes of old and new systems, may suffice. Second, netwar is not simply a function of the Internet; it does not take place only in cyberspace or the infosphere. Some key *battles* may occur there, but a *war's* overall conduct and outcome will normally depend mostly on what happens in the real world. Even in information-age conflicts, what happens in the real world is generally more important than what happens in the virtual worlds of cyberspace or the infosphere.[24] Netwar is not Internet war.

Swarming, and the Blurring of Offense and Defense

This distinctive, often ad-hoc design has unusual strengths, for both offense and defense. On the offense, networks are known for being adaptable, flexible, and versatile vis-à-vis opportunities and challenges. This may be particularly the case where a set of actors can engage in *swarming*. Little analytic attention has been given to swarming, yet it may be a key mode of conflict in the information age. The cutting edge for this possibility is found among netwar protagonists.[25]

Swarming occurs when the dispersed nodes of a network of small (and perhaps some large) forces converge on a target from multiple directions. The overall aim is the *sustainable pulsing* of force or fire. Once in motion, swarm networks must be able to coalesce rapidly and stealthily on a target, then dissever and redisperse, immediately ready to recombine for a new pulse. In other words, information-age

---

[24]See Paul Kneisel, "Netwar: The Battle Over Rec.Music.White-Power," *ANTIFA INFO-BULLETIN*, Research Supplement, June 12, 1996, unpaginated ASCII text available on the Internet. Kneisel analyzes the largest vote ever taken about the creation of a new Usenet newsgroup—a vote to prevent the creation of a group that was ostensibly about white-power music. He concludes that "The *war* against contemporary fascism will be won in the 'real world' off the net; but *battles* against fascist netwar are fought and won on the Internet." His title is testimony to the spreading usage of the term *netwar*.

[25]Swarm networks are discussed by Kevin Kelly, *Out of Control: The Rise of Neo-Biological Civilization*, A William Patrick Book, Addison-Wesley Publishing Company, New York, 1994. Also see Arquilla and Ronfeldt, 1997.

attacks may come in "swarms" rather than the more traditional "waves."

In terms of defensive potential, well-constructed networks tend to be redundant and diverse, making them robust and resilient in the face of adversity. Where they have a capacity for interoperability and shun centralized command and control, network designs can be difficult to crack and defeat as a whole. In particular, they may defy counterleadership targeting—attackers can find and confront only portions of the network. Moreover, the deniability built into a network may allow it to simply absorb a number of attacks on distributed nodes, leading the attacker to believe the network has been harmed when, in fact, it remains viable, and is seeking new opportunities for tactical surprise.

The difficulties of dealing with netwar actors deepen when the lines between offense and defense are blurred, or blended. When *blurring* is the case, it may be difficult to distinguish between attacking and defending actions, particularly when an actor goes on the offense in the name of self-defense. The *blending* of offense and defense will often mix the strategic and tactical levels of operations. For example, guerrillas on the defensive strategically may go on the offense tactically; the war of the *mujahideen* in Afghanistan provides a modern example.

The blurring of offense and defense reflects another feature of netwar: it tends to defy and cut across standard boundaries, jurisdictions, and distinctions between state and society, public and private, war and peace, war and crime, civilian and military, police and military, and legal and illegal. A government has difficulty assigning responsibility to a single agency—military, police, or intelligence—to respond.

Thus, the spread of netwar adds to the challenges facing the nation-state in the information age. Nation-state ideals of sovereignty and authority are traditionally linked to a bureaucratic rationality in which issues and problems can be neatly divided, and specific offices can be charged with taking care of specific problems. In netwar, things are rarely so clear. A protagonist is likely to operate in the cracks and gray areas of society, striking where lines of authority crisscross and the operational paradigms of politicians, officials, soldiers, police officers, and related actors get fuzzy and clash.

Networks Versus Hierarchies: Challenges for Counternetwar

Against this background, we are led to a set of four policy-oriented propositions about the information revolution and its implications for netwar and *counternetwar.*[26]

Hierarchies have a difficult time fighting networks. There are examples across the conflict spectrum. Some of the best are found in the failings of governments to defeat transnational criminal cartels engaged in drug smuggling, as in Colombia. The persistence of religious revivalist movements, as in Algeria, in the face of unremitting state opposition, shows the robustness of the network form. The Zapatista movement in Mexico, with its legions of supporters and sympathizers among local and transnational nongovernmental organizations (NGOs), shows that social netwar can put a democratizing autocracy on the defensive and pressure it to continue adopting reforms.

It takes networks to fight networks. Governments that would defend against netwar may have to adopt organizational designs and strategies like those of their adversaries. This does not mean mirroring the adversary, but rather learning to draw on the same design principles of network forms in the information age. These principles depend to some extent upon technological innovation, but mainly on a willingness to innovate organizationally and doctrinally, and by building new mechanisms for interagency and multijurisdictional cooperation.

Whoever masters the network form first and best will gain major advantages. In these early decades of the information age, adversaries who have adopted networking (be they criminals, terrorists, or peaceful social activists) are enjoying an increase in their power relative to state agencies.

---

[26]Also see Alexander Berger, "Organizational Innovation and Redesign in the Information Age: The Drug War, Netwar, and Other Low-End Conflict," Master's Thesis, Naval Postgraduate School, Monterey, California, 1998, for additional thinking and analysis about such propositions.

Counternetwar may thus require effective interagency approaches, which by their nature involve networked structures. The challenge will be to blend hierarchies and networks skillfully, while retaining enough core authority to encourage and enforce adherence to networked processes. By creating effective hybrids, governments may better confront the new threats and challenges emerging in the information age, whether generated by terrorists, militias, criminals, or other actors.[27] The U.S. Counterterrorist Center, based at the Central Intelligence Agency (CIA), is a good example of a promising effort to establish a functional interagency network,[28] although its success may depend increasingly on the strength of links with the military services and other institutions that fall outside the realm of the intelligence community.

MIDDLE EASTERN TERRORISM AND NETWAR

Terrorism seems to be evolving in the direction of violent netwar. Islamic fundamentalist organizations like Hamas and the bin Laden network consist of groups organized in loosely interconnected, semi-independent cells that have no single commanding hierarchy.[29] Hamas exemplifies the shift away from a hierarchically oriented

---

[27]For elaboration, see Arquilla and Ronfeldt, 1997, Chapter 19.

[28]Vernon Loeb, "Where the CIA Wages Its New World War," *Washington Post*, September 9, 1998. For a broader discussion of interagency cooperation in countering terrorism, see Ashton Carter, John Deutch, and Philip Zelikow, "Catastrophic Terrorism," *Foreign Affairs*, Vol. 77, No. 6, November/December 1998, pp. 80–94.

[29]Analogously, right-wing militias and extremist groups in the United States also rely on a doctrine of "leaderless resistance" propounded by Aryan nationalist Louis Beam. See Beam, 1992; and Kenneth Stern, *A Force upon the Plain: The American Militia Movement and the Politics of Hate*, Simon and Schuster, New York, 1996. Meanwhile, as part of a broader trend toward netwar, transnational criminal organizations (TCOs) have been shifting away from centralized "Dons" to more networked structures. See Phil Williams, "Transnational Criminal Organizations and International Security," *Survival*, Vol. 36, No. 1, Spring 1994, pp. 96–113; and Phil Williams, "The Nature of Drug-Trafficking Networks," *Current History*, April 1998, pp. 154–159. As noted earlier, social activist movements long ago began to evolve "segmented, polycephalous, integrated networks." For a discussion of a social netwar in which human-rights and other peaceful activist groups supported an insurgent group in Mexico, see David Ronfeldt and Armando Martinez, "A Comment on the Zapatista 'Netwar'," in John Arquilla and David Ronfeldt, 1997, pp. 369–391.

movement based on a "great leader" (like the PLO and Yasser Arafat).[30]

The netwar concept is consistent with patterns and trends in the Middle East, where the newer and more active terrorist groups appear to be adopting decentralized, flexible network structures. The rise of networked arrangements in terrorist organizations is part of a wider move away from formally organized, state-sponsored groups to privately financed, loose networks of individuals and subgroups that may have strategic guidance but enjoy tactical independence. Related to these shifts is the fact that terrorist groups are taking advantage of information technology to coordinate the activities of dispersed members. Such technology may be employed by terrorists not only to wage information warfare, but also to support their own networked organizations.[31]

While a comprehensive empirical analysis of the relationship between (a) the structure of terrorist organizations and (b) group activity or strength is beyond the scope of this paper,[32] a cursory examination of such a relationship among Middle Eastern groups offers some evidence to support the claim that terrorists are preparing to wage netwar. The Middle East was selected for analysis mainly be-

---

[30]It is important to differentiate our notions of information-age networking from earlier ideas about terror as consisting of a network in which all nodes revolved around a Soviet core (Claire Sterling, *The Terror Network,* Holt, Rinehart & Winston, New York, 1981). This view has generally been regarded as unsupported by available evidence (see Cindy C. Combs, *Terrorism in the Twenty-First Century,* Prentice-Hall, New York, 1997, pp. 99–119). However, there were a few early studies that did give credit to the possibility of the rise of terror networks that were bound more by loose ties to general strategic goals than by Soviet control (see especially Thomas L. Friedman, "Loose-Linked Network of Terror: Separate Acts, Ideological Bonds," *Terrorism,* Vol. 8, No. 1, Winter 1985, pp. 36–49).

[31]For good general background, see Michael Whine, "Islamist Organisations on the Internet," draft circulated on the Internet, April 1998 *(www.ict.org.il/articles).*

[32]We assume that group activity is a proxy for group strength. Group activity can be measured more easily than group strength, and is expected to be significantly correlated with strength. The relationship may not be perfect, but it is deemed to be sufficiently strong for our purposes.

cause terrorist groups based in this region have been active in targeting U.S. government facilities and interests, as in the bombings of
the Khobar Towers, and most recently, the American embassies in
Kenya and Tanzania.

Middle Eastern Terrorist Groups: Structure and Actions

Terrorist groups in the Middle East have diverse origins, ideologies,
and organizational structures, but can be roughly categorized into
traditional and new-generation groups. Traditional groups date back
to the late 1960s and early 1970s, and the majority of these were (and
some still are) formally or informally linked to the PLO. Typically,
they are also relatively bureaucratic and maintain a nationalist or
Marxist agenda. In contrast, most new-generation groups arose in
the 1980s and 1990s, have more fluid organizational forms, and rely
on Islam as a basis for their radical ideology.

The traditional, more-bureaucratic groups have survived to this day
partly through support from states such as Syria, Libya, and Iran.
The groups retain an ability to train and prepare for terrorist missions; however, their involvement in actual operations has been limited in recent years, partly because of successful counterterrorism
campaigns by Israeli and Western agencies. In contrast, the newer
and less hierarchical groups, such as Hamas, the Palestinian Islamic
Jihad (PIJ), Hizbullah, Algeria's Armed Islamic Group (GIA), the
Egyptian Islamic Group (IG), and Osama bin Laden's Arab Afghans,
have become the most active organizations in and around the
Middle East.

The traditional groups. Traditional terrorist groups in the Middle
East include the Abu Nidal Organization (ANO), the Popular Front
for the Liberation of Palestine (PFLP), and three PFLP-related
splinters—the PFLP-General Command (PFLP-GC), the Palestine
Liberation Front (PLF), and the Democratic Front for the Liberation
of Palestine (DFLP).

The ANO was an integral part of the PLO until it became independent in 1974. It has a bureaucratic structure composed of various

functional committees.[33] The activism it displayed in the 1970s and 1980s has lessened considerably, owing to a lessening of support from state sponsors and to effective counterterrorist campaigns by Israeli and Western intelligence services.[34] The very existence of the organization has recently been put into question, given uncertainty as to the whereabouts and fate of Abu Nidal, the leader of the group.[35]

The PFLP was founded in 1967 by George Habash as a PLO-affiliated organization. It has traditionally embraced a Marxist ideology, and remains an important PLO faction. However, in recent years it has suffered considerable losses from Israeli counterterrorist strikes.[36] The PFLP-General Command split from the PFLP in 1968, and in turn experienced a schism in the mid-1970s. This splinter group, which called itself the PLF, is composed of three subgroups, and has not been involved in high-profile acts since the 1985 hijacking of the Italian cruise ship *Achille Lauro*.[37] The PFLP was subjected to another split in 1969, which resulted in the Democratic Front for the Liberation of Palestine. The DFLP resembles a small army more than a terrorist group—its operatives are organized in battalions, backed by intelligence and special forces.[38] DFLP strikes have become less frequent since the 1970s, and since the late 1980s it has limited its attacks to Israeli targets near borders.[39]

What seems evident here is that this old generation of traditional, hierarchical, bureaucratic groups is on the wane. The reasons are varied, but the point remains—their way of waging terrorism is not likely to make a comeback, and is being superseded by a new way

---

[33]Office of the Coordinator for Counterterrorism, *Patterns of Global Terrorism, 1996,* U.S. Department of State, Publication 10433, April 1997.

[34]Loeb, 1998; and John Murray and Richard H. Ward (eds.), *Extremist Groups,* Office of International Criminal Justice, University of Illinois, Chicago, 1996.

[35]Youssef M. Ibrahim, "Egyptians Hold Terrorist Chief, Official Asserts," *New York Times,* August 26, 1998.

[36]Murray and Ward, 1996.

[37]*Patterns of Global Terrorism, 1996,* and Murray and Ward, 1996.

[38]Murray and Ward, 1996.

[39]*Patterns of Global Terrorism, 1995, 1996, 1997.*

that is more attuned to the organizational, doctrinal, and technological imperatives of the information age.

The most active groups and their organization. The new generation of Middle Eastern groups has been active both in and outside the region in recent years. In Israel and the occupied territories, Hamas, and to a lesser extent the Palestinian Islamic Jihad, have shown their strength over the last four years with a series of suicide bombings that have killed more than one hundred people and injured several more.[40] Exploiting a strong presence in Lebanon, the Shi'ite Hizbullah organization has also staged a number of attacks against Israeli Defense Forces troops and Israeli cities in Galilee.[41]

The al-Gama'a al-Islamiya, or Islamic Group (IG), is the most active Islamic extremist group in Egypt. In November 1997 IG carried out an attack on Hatshepsut's Temple in Luxor, killing 58 tourists and 4 Egyptians. The Group has also claimed responsibility for the bombing of the Egyptian embassy in Islamabad, Pakistan, which left 16 dead and 60 injured.[42] In Algeria, the Armed Islamic Group (GIA) has been behind the most violent, lethal attacks in Algeria's protracted civil war. Approximately 70,000 Algerians have lost their lives since the domestic terrorist campaign began in 1992.[43]

Recently, the loosely organized group of Arab Afghans—radical Islamic fighters from several North African and Middle Eastern countries who forged ties while resisting the Soviet occupation of

---

[40]For instance, in 1997 Hamas operatives set off three suicide bombs in crowded public places in Tel Aviv and Jerusalem. On March 21, a Hamas satchel bomb exploded at a Tel Aviv cafe, killing three persons and injuring 48; on July 30, two Hamas suicide bombers blew themselves up in a Jerusalem market, killing 16 persons and wounding 178; on September 4, three suicide bombers attacked a Jerusalem pedestrian mall, killing at least five persons (in addition to the suicide bombers), and injuring at least 181. The Palestinian Islamic Jihad has claimed responsibility (along with Hamas) for a bomb that killed 20 and injured 75 others in March 1996, and in 1995 it carried out five bombings that killed 29 persons and wounded 107. See *Patterns of Global Terrorism, 1995, 1996, 1997.*

[41]See "Hizbullah," Israeli Foreign Ministry, April 11, 1996. Available on the Internet at *http://www.israel-mfa.gov.il.*

[42]See *Patterns of Global Terrorism, 1995, 1996, 1997.*

[43]*Patterns of Global Terrorism, 1997.*

Afghanistan[44]—has come to the fore as an active terrorist outfit. One of the leaders and founders of the Arab Afghan movement, Osama bin Laden, a Saudi entrepreneur who bases his activities in Afghanistan,[45] is suspected of sending operatives to Yemen to bomb a hotel used by U.S. soldiers on their way to Somalia in 1992, plotting to assassinate President Clinton in the Philippines in 1994 and Egyptian President Hosni Mubarak in 1995, and of having a role in the Riyadh and Khobar blasts in Saudi Arabia that resulted in the deaths of 24 Americans in 1995 and 1996.[46] U.S. officials have pointed to bin Laden as the mastermind behind the U.S. embassy bombings in Kenya and Tanzania, which claimed the lives of more than 260 people, including 12 Americans.[47]

To varying degrees, these groups share the principles of the networked organization—relatively flat hierarchies, decentralization and delegation of decisionmaking authority, and loose lateral ties among dispersed groups and individuals.[48] For instance, Hamas is loosely structured, with some elements working openly through mosques and social service institutions to recruit members, raise funds, organize activities, and distribute propaganda. Palestinian security sources indicate that there are ten or more Hamas splinter groups and factions with no centralized operational leadership.[49] The Palestine Islamic Jihad is a series of loosely affiliated factions,

---

[44]"Arab Afghans Said to Launch Worldwide Terrorist War," *Paris al-Watan al-'Arabi,* FBIS-TOT-96-010-L, December 1, 1995, pp. 22–24.

[45]William Gertz, "Saudi Financier Tied to Attacks," *Washington Times,* October 23, 1996.

[46]Tim Weiner, "U.S. Sees bin Laden as Ringleader of Terrorist Network," *New York Times,* August 21, 1998; M. J. Zuckerman, "Bin Laden Indicted for Bid to Kill Clinton," *USA Today,* August 26, 1998.

[47]Pamela Constable, "bin Laden 'Is Our Guest, So We Must Protect Him'," *Washington Post,* August 21, 1998.

[48]We distinguish between deliberate and factional decentralization. Factional decentralization—prevalent in older groups—occurs when subgroups separate themselves from the central leadership because of differences in tactics or approach. Deliberate or operational decentralization is what distinguishes netwar agents from others, since delegation of authority in this case occurs because of the distinct advantages this organizational arrangement brings, and not because of lack of consensus. We expect both influences on decentralization to continue, but newer groups will tend to decentralize authority even in the absence of political disagreements.

[49]"Gaza Strip, West Bank; Dahlan on Relations with Israel, Terrorism," *Tel Aviv Yedi'ot Aharonot,* FBIS-TOT-97-022-L, February 28, 1997, p. 18.

rather than a cohesive group.[50] The pro-Iranian Hizbullah acts as an umbrella organization of radical Shiite groups, and in many respects is a hybrid of hierarchical and network arrangements; Although the formal structure is highly bureaucratic, interactions among members are volatile and do not follow rigid lines of control.[51] According to the U.S. Department of State, Egypt's Islamic Group is a decentralized organization that operates without a single operational leader,[52] while the GIA is notorious for the lack of centralized authority.[53]

Unlike traditional terrorist organizations, Arab Afghans are part of a complex network of relatively autonomous groups that are financed from private sources forming "a kind of international terrorists' Internet."[54] The most notorious element of the network is Osama bin Laden, who uses his wealth and organizational skills to support and direct a multinational alliance of Islamic extremists. At the heart of this alliance is his own inner core group, known as Al-Qaeda ("The Base"), which sometimes conducts missions on its own, but more often in conjunction with other groups or elements in the alliance. The goal of the alliance is opposition on a global scale to perceived threats to Islam, as indicated by bin Laden's 1996 declaration of a holy war against the United States and the West. In the document, bin Laden specifies that such a holy war will be fought by irregular, light, highly mobile forces using guerrilla tactics.[55]

---

[50]The leader of the PIJ's most powerful faction, Fathi Shaqaqi, was assassinated in October 1995 in Malta, allegedly by the Israeli Mossad. Shaqaqi's killing followed the assassination of Hani Abed, another PIJ leader killed in 1994 in Gaza. Reports that the group has been considerably weakened as a result of Israeli counterleadership operations are balanced by the strength demonstrated by the PIJ in its recent terrorist activity. See "Islamic Group Vows Revenge for Slaying of Its Leader," *New York Times*, October 30, 1995, p. 9.

[51]Magnus Ranstorp, "Hizbullah's Command Leadership: Its Structure, Decision-Making and Relationship with Iranian Clergy and Institutions," *Terrorism and Political Violence*, Vol. 6, No. 3, Autumn 1994, p. 304.

[52]*Patterns of Global Terrorism, 1996.*

[53]"Algeria: Infighting Among Proliferating 'Wings' of Armed Groups," *London al-Sharq al-Aswat*, FBIS-TOT-97-021-L, February 24, 1997, p. 4.

[54]David B. Ottaway, "US Considers Slugging It Out With International Terrorism," *Washington Post*, October 17, 1996, p. 25.

[55]"Saudi Arabia: Bin-Laden Calls for 'Guerrilla Warfare' Against US Forces," *Beirut Al-Diyar*, FBIS-NES-96-180, September 12, 1996.

Even though bin Laden finances Arab Afghan activities and directs some operations, he apparently does not play a direct command and control role over all operatives. Rather, he is a key figure in the co-ordination and support of several dispersed activities.[56] For instance, bin Laden founded the "World Islamic Front for Jihad Against Jews and Crusaders."[57] And yet most of the groups that participate in this front (including Egypt's Islamic Group) remain independent, although the organizational barriers between them are fluid.[58]

From a netwar perspective, an interesting feature of bin Laden's Arab Afghan movement is its ability to relocate operations swiftly from one geographic area to another in response to changing circumstances and needs. Arab Afghans have participated in operations conducted by Algeria's GIA and Egypt's IG. Reports in 1997 also indicated that Arab Afghans transferred training operations to Somalia, where they joined the Islamic Liberation Party (ILP).[59] The same reports suggest that the Arab Afghan movement has considered sending fighters to Sinkiang Uighur province in western China, to wage a holy war against the Chinese regime.[60] This group's ability to move and act quickly (and, to some extent, to swarm) once opportunities emerge hampers counterterrorist efforts to predict its actions and monitor its activities. The fact that Arab Afghan operatives were able to strike the U.S. embassies in Kenya and Tanzania substantiates the claim that members of this network have the mobility and speed to operate over considerable distances.

---

[56]It is important to avoid equating the bin Laden network solely with bin Laden. He represents a key node in the Arab Afghan terror network, but there should be no illusions about the likely effect on the network of actions taken to neutralize him. The network conducts many operations without his involvement, leadership, or financing—and will continue to be able to do so should he be killed or captured.

[57]"Militants Say There Will Be More Attacks Against U.S.," *European Stars and Stripes*, August 20, 1998.

[58]For instance, there have been reports of a recent inflow of Arab Afghans into Egypt's Islamic Group to reinforce the latter's operations. See Murray and Ward, 1996, and "The CIA on Bin Laden," *Foreign Report*, No. 2510, August 27, 1998, pp. 2–3.

[59]This move was also influenced by the Taliban's decision to curb Arab Afghan activities in the territory under its control as a result of U.S. pressure. See "Arab Afghans Reportedly Transfer Operations to Somalia," *Cairo al-Arabi*, FBIS-TOT-97-073, March 10, 1997, p. 1.

[60]"Afghanistan, China: Report on Bin-Laden Possibly Moving to China," *Paris al-Watan al 'Arabi*, FBIS-NES-97-102, May 23, 1997, pp. 19–20.

Although the organizational arrangements in these groups do not match all the basic features of the network ideal,[61] they stand in contrast to more traditional groups. Another feature that distinguishes the newer generation of terrorist groups is their adoption of information technology.

Middle Eastern Terrorist Groups and the Use of Information Technology

Information technology (IT) is an enabling factor for networked groups; terrorists aiming to wage netwar may adopt it not only as a weapon, but also to help coordinate and support their activities. Before exploring how Middle Eastern terrorist groups have embraced the new technology, we posit three hypotheses that relate the rise of IT to organization for netwar:

- The greater the degree of organizational networking in a terrorist group, the higher the likelihood that IT is used to support the network's decisionmaking.

- Recent advances in IT facilitate networked terrorist organizations because information flows are becoming quicker, cheaper, more secure, and more versatile.

- As terrorist groups learn to use IT for decisionmaking and other organizational purposes, they will be likely to use the same technology as an offensive weapon to destroy or disrupt.

Middle Eastern terrorist groups provide examples of information technology being used for a wide variety of purposes. As discussed below, there is some evidence to support the claim that the most active groups—and therefore the most decentralized groups—have embraced information technology to coordinate activities and dis-

---

[61]While it is possible to discern a general trend toward an organizational structure that displays several features of a network, we expect to observe substantial differences (and many hierarchy/network hybrids) in how organizations make their specific design choices. Different network designs depend on contingent factors, such as personalities, organizational history, operational requirements, and other influences such as state sponsorship and ideology.

seminate propaganda and ideology.[62] At the same time, the technical assets and know-how gained by terrorist groups as they seek to form into multi-organizational networks can be used for offensive purposes—an Internet connection can be used for both coordination and disruption. The anecdotes provided here are consistent with the rise in the Middle East of what has been termed *techno-terrorism*, or the use by terrorists of satellite communications, e-mail, and the World Wide Web.[63]

Arab Afghans appear to have widely adopted information technology. According to reporters who visited bin Laden's headquarters in a remote mountainous area of Afghanistan, the terrorist financier has computers, communications equipment, and a large number of disks for data storage.[64] Egyptian "Afghan" computer experts are said to have helped devise a communication network that relies on the World Wide Web, e-mail, and electronic bulletin boards so that the extremists can exchange information without running a major risk of being intercepted by counterterrorism officials.[65]

Hamas is another major group that uses the Internet to share operational information. Hamas activists in the United States use chat rooms to plan operations and activities.[66] Operatives use e-mail to coordinate activities across Gaza, the West Bank, and Lebanon. Hamas has realized that information can be passed securely over the Internet because it is next to impossible for counterterrorism intelli-

---

[62]Assessing the strength of the relationship between organizational structure and use of information technology is difficult to establish. Alternative explanations may exist as to why newer groups would embrace information technology, such as age of the group (one could speculate that newer terrorist groups have on average younger members, who are more familiar with computers), or the amount of funding (a richer group could afford more electronic gadgetry). While it is empirically impossible to refute these points, much in organization theory supports our hypothesis that there is a direct relationship between a higher need for information technology and the use of network structures.

[63]"Saudi Arabia: French Analysis of Islamic Threat," *Paris al-Watan al-'Arabi*, FBIS-NES-97-082, April 11, 1997, pp. 4–8.

[64]"Afghanistan, Saudi Arabia: Editor's Journey to Meet Bin-Laden Described," *London al-Quds al-'Arabi*, FBIS-TOT-97-003-L, November 27, 1996, p. 4.

[65]"Arab Afghans Said to Launch Worldwide Terrorist War," 1995.

[66]"Israel: U.S. Hamas Activists Use Internet to Send Attack Threats," *Tel Aviv IDF Radio*, FBIS-TOT-97-001-L, 0500 GMT October 13, 1996.

gence to monitor accurately the flow and content of Internet traffic. Israeli security officials have difficulty in tracing Hamas messages and decoding their content.[67]

During a recent counterterrorist operation, several GIA bases in Italy were uncovered, and each was found to include computers and diskettes with instructions for the construction of bombs.[68] It has been reported that the GIA uses floppy disks and computers to store and process instructions and other information for its members, who are dispersed in Algeria and Europe.[69] Furthermore, the Internet is used as a propaganda tool by Hizbullah, which manages three World Wide Web sites—one for the central press office (at www.hizbollah.org), another to describe its attacks on Israeli targets (at www.moqawama.org), and the last for news and information (at www.almanar.com.lb).[70]

The presence of Middle Eastern terrorist organizations on the Internet is suspected in the case of the Islamic Gateway, a World Wide Web site that contains information on a number of Islamic activist organizations based in the United Kingdom. British Islamic activists use the World Wide Web to broadcast their news and attract funding; they are also turning to the Internet as an organizational and communication tool.[71] While the vast majority of Islamic activist groups represented in the Islamic Gateway are legitimate, one group—the Global Jihad Fund—makes no secret of its militant goals.[72] The appeal of the Islamic Gateway for militant groups may be enhanced by a representative's claim, in an Internet Newsnet article in August 1996, that the Gateway's Internet Service Provider

---

[67]"Israel: Hamas Using Internet to Relay Operational Messages," *Tel Aviv Ha'aretz*, FBIS-TOT-98-034, February 3, 1998, p. 1.

[68]"Italy: Security Alters Following Algerian Extremists' Arrests," *Milan Il Giornale*, FBIS-TOT-97-002-L, November 12, 1996, p. 10.

[69]"Italy, Vatican City: Daily Claims GIA 'Strategist' Based in Milan," *Milan Corriere della Sera*, FBIS-TOT-97-004-L, December 5, 1996, p. 9.

[70]"Hizbullah TV Summary 18 February 1998," *Al-Manar Television World Wide Webcast*, FBIS-NES-98-050, February 19, 1998. Also see "Developments in Mideast Media: January–May 1998," Foreign Broadcast Information Service (FBIS), May 11, 1998.

[71]"Islamists on Internet," FBIS Foreign Media Note-065EP96, September 9, 1996.

[72]"Islamic Activism Online," FBIS Foreign Media Note-02JAN97, January 3, 1997.

(ISP) can give "CIA-proof" protection against electronic surveillance.[73]

Summary Comment

This review of patterns and trends in the Middle East substantiates our speculations that the new terrorism is evolving in the direction of netwar, along the following lines:[74]

- An increasing number of terrorist groups are adopting networked forms of organization and relying on information technology to support such structures.

- Newer groups (those established in the 1980s and 1990s) are more networked than traditional groups.

- A positive correlation is emerging between the degree of activity of a group and the degree to which it adopts a networked structure.[75]

- Information technology is as likely to be used for organizational support as for offensive warfare.

- The likelihood that young recruits will be familiar with information technology implies that terrorist groups will be increasingly

---

[73]The Muslim Parliament has recently added an Internet Relay Chat (IRC) link and a "Muslims only" List-Serve (automatic e-mail delivery service). See "Islamic Activism Online," FBIS Foreign Media Note-02JAN97, January 3, 1997.

[74]Similar propositions may apply to varieties of netwar other than the new terrorism.

[75]We make a qualification here. There appears to be a significant positive association between the degree to which a group is active and the degree to which a group is decentralized and networked. But we cannot be confident about the causality of this relationship or its direction (i.e., whether activity and strength affect networking, or vice-versa). A host of confounding factors may affect both the way groups decide to organize and their relative success at operations. For instance, the age of a group may be an important predictor of a group's success—newer groups are likely to be more popular; popular groups are more likely to enlist new operatives; and groups that have a large number of operatives are likely to be more active, regardless of organizational structure. Another important caveat is related to the fact that it is difficult to rank groups precisely in terms of the degree to which they are networked, because no terrorist organization is thought to represent either a hierarchical or network ideal-type. While the conceptual division between newer-generation and traditional groups is appropriate for our scope here, an analytical "degree of networking" scale would have to be devised for more empirical research.

networked and more computer-friendly in the future than they are today.

TERRORIST DOCTRINES—THE RISE OF A "WAR PARADIGM"

The evolution of terrorism in the direction of netwar will create new difficulties for counterterrorism. The types of challenges, and their severity, will depend on the kinds of doctrines that terrorists develop and employ. Some doctrinal effects will occur at the operational level, as in the relative emphasis placed on disruptive information operations as distinct from destructive combat operations. However, at a deeper level, the direction in which terrorist netwar evolves will depend upon the choices terrorists make as to the overall doctrinal paradigms that shape their goals and strategies.

At least three terrorist paradigms are worth considering: terror as coercive diplomacy, terror as war, and terror as the harbinger of a "new world." These three engage, in varying ways, distinct rationales for terrorism—as a weapon of the weak, as a way to assert identity, and as a way to break through to a new world—discussed earlier in this chapter. While there has been much debate about the overall success or failure of terrorism,[76] the paradigm under which a terrorist operates may have a great deal to do with the likelihood of success. Coercion, for example, implies distinctive threats or uses of force, whereas norms of "war" often imply maximizing destruction.

The Coercive-Diplomacy Paradigm

The first paradigm is that of coercive diplomacy. From its earliest days, terrorism has often sought to persuade others, by means of symbolic violence, either to do something, stop doing something, or undo what has been done. These are the basic forms of coercive diplomacy,[77] and they appear in terrorism as far back as the Jewish

---

[76]See, for instance, William Gutteridge (ed.), *Contemporary Terrorism*, Facts on File, Oxford, England, 1986; Hoffman and Carr, 1997; and Combs, 1997.

[77]See Alexander George and William Simons, *The Limits of Coercive Diplomacy*, Westview Press, Boulder, 1994.

Sicarii Zealots who sought independence from Rome in the first century AD, up through the Palestinians' often violent acts in pursuit of their independence today.

The fact that terrorist coercion includes violent acts does not make it a form of war—the violence is exemplary, designed to encourage what Alexander George calls "forceful persuasion," or "coercive diplomacy as an alternative to war."[78] In this light, terrorism may be viewed as designed to achieve specific goals, and the level of violence is limited, or proportional, to the ends being pursued. Under this paradigm, terrorism was once thought to lack a "demand" for WMD, as such tools would provide means vastly disproportionate to the ends of terror. This view was first elucidated over twenty years ago by Brian Jenkins—though there was some dissent expressed by scholars such as Thomas Schelling—and continued to hold sway until a few years ago.[79]

The War Paradigm

Caleb Carr, surveying the history of the failures of coercive terrorism and the recent trends toward increasing destructiveness and deniability, has elucidated what we call a "war paradigm."[80] This paradigm, which builds on ideas first considered by Jenkins,[81] holds that terrorist acts arise when weaker parties cannot challenge an adversary directly and thus turn to asymmetric methods. A war paradigm implies taking a strategic, campaign-oriented view of violence that makes no specific call for concessions from, or other demands upon, the opponent. Instead, the strategic aim is to inflict damage, in the context of what the terrorists view as an ongoing war. In theory, this paradigm, unlike the coercive diplomacy one, does not seek a proportional relationship between the level of force em-

---

[78]Alexander George, *Forceful Persuasion: Coercive Diplomacy as an Alternative to War,* United States Institute of Peace Press, Washington, DC, 1991.

[79]Brian Jenkins, *The Potential for Nuclear Terrorism,* RAND, P-5876, 1977; Thomas Schelling, "Thinking about Nuclear Terrorism," *International Security,* Vol. 6, No. 4, Spring 1982, pp. 68–75; and Patrick Garrity and Steven Maaranen, *Nuclear Weapons in a Changing World,* Plenum Press, New York, 1992.

[80]Carr, 1996.

[81]Brian Jenkins, *International Terrorism: A New Kind of Warfare,* RAND, P-5261, 1974.

ployed and the aims sought. When the goal is to inflict damage generally, and the terrorist group has no desire or need to claim credit, there is an attenuation of the need for proportionality—the worse the damage, the better. Thus, the use of WMD can be far more easily contemplated than in a frame of reference governed by notions of coercive diplomacy.

A terrorist war paradigm may be undertaken by terrorists acting on their own behalf or in service to a nation-state. In the future, as the information age brings the further empowerment of nonstate and transnational actors, "stateless" versions of the terrorist war paradigm may spread. At the same time, however, states will remain important players in the war paradigm; they may cultivate their own terrorist-style commandos, or seek cut-outs and proxies from among nonstate terrorist groups.

Ambiguity regarding a sponsor's identity may prove a key element of the war paradigm. While the use of proxies provides an insulating layer between a state sponsor and its target, these proxies, if captured, may prove more susceptible to interrogation and investigative techniques designed to winkle out the identity of the sponsor. On the other hand, while home-grown commando-style terrorists may be less forthcoming with information if caught, their own identities, which may be hard to conceal, may provide undeniable evidence of state sponsorship. These risks for states who think about engaging in or supporting terrorism may provide yet more reason for the war paradigm to increasingly become the province of nonstate terrorists—or those with only the most tenuous linkages to particular states.

Exemplars of the war paradigm today are the wealthy Saudi jihadist, Osama bin Laden, and the Arab Afghans that he associates with. As previously mentioned, bin Laden has explicitly called for war-like terrorism against the United States, and especially against U.S. military forces stationed in Saudi Arabia. President Clinton's statement that American retaliation for the U.S. embassy bombings in East Africa represented the first shots in a protracted war on terrorism suggests that the notion of adopting a war paradigm to counter terror has gained currency.

The New-World Paradigm

A third terrorist paradigm aims at achieving the birth of what might be called a "new world." It may be driven by religious mania, a desire for totalitarian control, or an impulse toward ultimate chaos.[82] Aum Shinrikyo would be a recent example. The paradigm harks back to the dynamics of millennialist movements that arose in past epochs of social upheaval, when *prophetae* attracted adherents from the margins of other social movements and led small groups to pursue salvation by seeking a final, violent cataclysm.[83]

This paradigm is likely to seek the vast disruption of political, social, and economic order. Accomplishing this goal may involve lethal de struction, even a heightened willingness to use WMD. Religious terrorists may desire destruction for its own sake, or for some form of "cleansing." But the ultimate aim is not so much the destruction of society as a rebirth after a period of chaotic disruption.

The Paradigms and Netwar

All three paradigms offer room for netwar. Moreover, all three paradigms allow the rise of "cybotage"—acts of disruption and destruction against information infrastructures by terrorists who learn the skills of cyberterror, as well as by disaffected individuals with technical skills who are drawn into the terrorist milieu. However, we note that terrorist netwar may also be a battle of ideas—and to wage this form of conflict some terrorists may want the Net *up*, not down.

Many experts argue that terrorism is moving toward ever more lethal, destructive acts. Our netwar perspective accepts this, but also holds that some terrorist netwars will stress disruption over destruction. Networked terrorists will no doubt continue to destroy things and kill people, but their principal strategy may move toward the nonlethal

---

[82]For a discussion of these motives, see Laqueur, 1996; Iklé, 1997; and Hoffman, 1998, respectively.

[83]See, for instance, Michael Barkun, *Disaster and the Millennium*, Yale University Press, New Haven, 1974; and Norman Cohn, *The Pursuit of the Millennium: Revolutionary Messianism in Medieval and Reformation Europe and Its Bearing on Modern Totalitarian Movements*, Harper Torch Books, New York, 1961.

end of the spectrum, where command and control nodes and vulnerable information infrastructures provide rich sets of targets.

Indeed, terrorism has long been about "information"—from the fact that trainees for suicide bombings are kept from listening to international media, through the ways that terrorists seek to create disasters that will consume the front pages, to the related debates about countermeasures that would limit freedom of the press, increase public surveillance and intelligence gathering, and heighten security over information and communications systems. Terrorist tactics focus attention on the importance of information and communications for the functioning of democratic institutions; debates about how terrorist threats undermine democratic practices may revolve around freedom of information issues.

While netwar may be waged by terrorist groups operating with any of the three paradigms, the rise of networked groups whose objective is to wage war may be the one most relevant to and dangerous from the standpoint of the military. Indeed, if terrorists perceive themselves as warriors, they may be inclined to target enemy military assets or interests.

INFORMATION-AGE TERRORISM AND THE U.S. AIR FORCE

Terrorists, especially those operating under a war paradigm, have every reason to seek out and target U.S. military personnel, installations, and equipment. The inability to pose direct opposition to American power may stimulate ethno-nationalist and religious revivalist movements—both types of actors may feel inherently threatened by the preeminent position of the United States in current world politics. Using a war paradigm allows terrorists an easy rationale for striking at American power, even in the absence of specific demands and without the need to claim credit for actions. Further, the high profile of the Air Force suggests that attacks upon it will be a way to grab worldwide public attention and strike at what is perceived, by some, to be a "conditionally fragile" American public ability to accept losses and casualties.[84]

---

[84]Eric V. Larson, *Casualties and Consensus: The Historical Role of Casualties in Domestic Support for U.S. Military Operations*, RAND, MR-726-RC, 1996.

The U.S. Air Force, which in many ways epitomizes American power—as the Royal Navy did in the heyday of British Empire—has symbolic value as a target of terror. It also has expensive and sophisticated equipment that increases its attractiveness to the terrorist. Further, air assets are a quintessential element of the balance of power in any region of the world, as they are an available form of American military power that may be exercised in support of U.S. interests. Given a U.S. air mastery that precludes direct challenges, a terrorist commando strategy against U.S. air assets might prove an attractive option for potential adversaries.

This option poses the prospect of a campaign with low costs and risks—much like the British use of the Special Air Service (SAS) in North Africa during World War II. In that campaign, British commandos were sent against Luftwaffe airbases, destroying over 400 aircraft between 1941 and 1943 and helping to mitigate the effects of German air superiority early in the desert war with deep strikes of up to 400 miles behind the front.[85] This irregular approach to weakening an enemy's air power has remained a vibrant strand in British strategic thought, and the SAS would reprise its role in the 1982 Falklands War, most notably by destroying 11 Argentine ground-attack aircraft in the raid on Pebble Island.[86] The potential of this type of threat to USAF bases has been acknowledged, and mitigation measures explored, in recent studies on ground-based threats to airbases.[87]

For the USAF, the prospect of terrorist attack exists across the spectrum of operations and across the types of asset—from personnel to equipment, and, increasingly, against command and control nodes.

---

[85]Paul Carell, *The Foxes of the Desert*, E. P. Dutton, New York, 1960, pp. 47–49.

[86]See Max Hastings and Simon Jenkins, *The Battle for the Falklands*, W. W. Norton, New York, 1983, pp. 186–187; Anthony Cordesmann, and Abraham Wagner, *The Lessons of Modern War*, Vol. 3, *The Afghan and Falklands Conflicts*, Westview Press, Boulder, Colorado, 1990. p. 305; and Bruce W. Watson and Peter M. Dunn (eds.), *Military Lessons of the Falklands Islands War*, Westview Press, Boulder, Colorado, 1984, pp. 153–154. For a comprehensive study of ground attacks on airbases, see Alan Vick, *Snakes in the Eagle's Nest: A History of Ground Attacks on Air Bases*, RAND, MR-553-AF, 1995, who chronicles the events that resulted in destruction of over 2000 aircraft on the ground between 1940 and 1992.

[87]See David A. Shlapak and Alan Vick, *Check Six Begins on the Ground: Responding to the Evolving Ground Threat to U.S. Air Force Bases*, RAND, MR-606-AF, 1995.

In peacetime, for example, the USAF plays a key role in maintaining a sense of American presence around the world. It is often a part of shows of force, and is an element in the American grand strategy of being open to the world regarding its military prowess—an important part of extending deterrent protection to U.S. friends and allies. Small-scale contingencies (SSC) range, on their lower-intensity end of the spectrum, from humanitarian aid delivery to peace enforcement (e.g., of "no fly" zones). Finally, the USAF will always play a key role in major theater wars (MTW), shoring up indigenous forces and multiplying the strength of other American military forces arriving in theater. U.S. air power, in this last category, may be the only viable hope of slowing down a numerically superior aggressor—and the aggressor may realize this, raising his interest in a terrorist commando strategy against the USAF.

Toward a New USAF Strategy for Coping with Information-Age Terrorism

At the most basic level, USAF strategy needs to have both defensive (antiterrorist) and proactive (counterterrorist) components. Measures must be devised to protect forces stationed at home and abroad, to strike targets belonging to groups or their sponsors, and to gather intelligence on imminent attacks or other terrorist group activities. More specifically, the USAF strategy against terrorism should encompass four generic missions:

- General, "political" deterrence
- Interdiction and strike
- Intelligence gathering
- Force protection.

General deterrence relates to the USAF's ability to prevent further terrorist actions by striking (or threatening to strike) those targets of most value to the political supporters of a given group; interdiction and strike refer to the tactical use of USAF assets in the pursuit of terrorist attackers, as well as for retaliatory response. Intelligence gathering finds information about imminent terrorist attacks and identifies terrorist group weaknesses. As its name suggests, force protection concerns the security and safety of USAF personnel, plants, and equipment.

Each mission has different implications for how the Air Force responds to the terrorist threat. Greater emphasis on force protection, for instance, would place more weight on defensive antiterrorism. The deterrence and strike missions are inherently more proactive, while intelligence gathering can serve the causes of both anti- and counterterrorism.

The foregoing suggests that the USAF should adopt a balanced approach that emphasizes all four missions to achieve an offensive/ defensive blend that can defend against and counter information-age terrorism.

Mitigation Measures

The USAF must devise measures to protect personnel, equipment and installations, and C2 nodes.

First, in the face of a significant increase in terrorist attacks (conventional or WMD) on USAF personnel and assets overseas, the USAF might consider shifting away from forward basing as much as possible, returning to forces based in the continental United States (CONUS) but with a wide network of dormant bases in the regions of interest. The principle here is similar to that articulated by Albert Wohlstetter et al. in their classic study of forward-based bomber vulnerability to surprise attack—the further forward, the more vulnerable the bombers.[88] In the future, if the terrorist threat grows substantially, a similar basing solution might be applicable. Such an option would dovetail neatly with emerging USAF doctrine regarding the surging forward of air expeditionary forces in crisis and war. While it may be difficult to secure access to a large number of bases, the redundancy created by this option would make it difficult for terrorists to predict which dormant bases to target prior to a deployment, and would help the USAF to remain engaged in key regions through "virtual presence."

---

[88]Albert Wohlstetter, F. Hoffman, R. J. Lutz, and H. S. Rowen, *Selection and Use of Strategic Air Bases*, RAND, R-266, 1954.

As attractive as moving to a preponderantly CONUS-based force might be under some circumstances, it would present a number of problems. First, there would be costs and risks to regional stability engendered by a lack of U.S. presence. For example, the USAF has been the principal stabilizer for Kuwait in the Persian Gulf region since the end of the war. Air assets are often crucial for deterrence and defense; when deterrence fails, it takes time to muster American ground and naval forces for a response. Therefore, when forward basing is deemed absolutely necessary for crisis stability, or for peace operations (e.g., "no fly" zones), the host nation must be made aware of USAF security requirements and allow the USAF an active role in preparing its antiterrorist defenses.

Also, the USAF might explore developing standardized doctrine regarding antiterrorism—perhaps along the lines of the general guidance that is provided by the Joint Staff.[89] Clearly, different regional settings impose differing security requirements, but the USAF can develop a body of generalizable thought to impart to base commanders and others charged with securing USAF assets and personnel overseas. Our research has revealed a wide variance in views about base and personnel security, as well as widely differing levels of concern about the problem.

With regard to forward basing, one must consider the risk of terrorist attack on prepositioned supplies and ordnance. The simplest solution is to move as much prepositioned equipment out to sea as possible, a step that the USAF has already partially taken. However, this approach then subjects the USAF to the same problem that the U.S. Navy has in terms of response time—the need to wait for the arrival of ships, which will, generally, take some days to reach the region in question. Depending on the weakness of the American ally in the regional setting, a delay of days can be critical. Maritime prepositioning squadrons will not provide an overall solution, but they may provide a useful hedge in a prepositioning scheme that includes both ground-based materials and those kept afloat.[90]

---

[89]Joint Staff, *Joint Tactics, Techniques and Procedures for Antiterrorism*, JP 3-07.2, March 1998.

[90]On the theme of maritime prepositioning, it might also be useful to think about the concept of mobile, floating airbases. These would be like the mobile, large islands (MOLIs) first discussed during the Cold War (see P. M. Dadant, A. A. Barbour, W. E.

The second deficiency with CONUS-basing as a solution lies in the nature of terrorist IW, which is not limited by geographical concerns. Indeed, in some respects, the highly internetted U.S. information infrastructure might make access to USAF C2 nodes easier than if an airbase were located in the northern desert of Saudi Arabia. How, then, should the terrorist information warfare threat be defended against? A simple solution is to avoid becoming too interconnected to the global information infrastructure. The USAF currently retains the robust, dedicated C2 system that it needed to operate under the most trying conditions (i.e., protracted nuclear war), so perhaps the answer lies in *not* interconnecting all sensitive communications as rapidly as possible. Paradoxically, less modernization may make for more security in some cases.

Moving toward more advanced electronic interconnectivity might undermine the security and safety of the current system, opening up a window of opportunity for cyberterror. The problem of increasing modernization and complexity is noted by Perrow and Sagan.[91]

Proactive Counterterrorism and the USAF

If terrorists are moving toward a war paradigm, then it may be appropriate for the targeted to move to a war paradigm of their own. Indeed, President Clinton deliberately invoked the language and imagery of a war paradigm in his public comments on the reasons for retaliating with missile attacks against the terrorists responsible for the 1998 U.S. embassy bombings in East Africa. The adoption of a war paradigm by the U.S. armed forces would carry deep political

---

Mooz, and J. K. Walker, *A Comparison of Methods for Improving U.S. Capability to Project Ground Forces to Southwest Asia in the 1990s*, RAND, R-2963-AF, 1984) that were envisioned to have a movement capability of some three knots per hour. MOLIs would solve the problem of where to preposition supplies, and they would reduce the vulnerability of forward-based air power to terrorist attack. MOLIs are limited to the sea, so airbases would necessarily have inherent limits on their placement. MOLIs could defend against some forms of terrorist attack but might be lucrative targets of assault by regional navies using swift missile boats. Finally, the MOLI could be an attractive target for a tactical WMD. Despite its weaknesses, the MOLI concept might have more appeal in the case of a substantial rise in terrorist activity, or in those areas where local military and WMD threats are deemed low.

[91]Charles Perrow, *Normal Accidents: Living with High-Risk Technologies*, Basic Books, New York, 1984, and Scott D. Sagan, *The Limits of Safety: Organizations, Accidents, and Nuclear Weapons*, Princeton University Press, Princeton, New Jersey, 1993.

and security implications, especially in terms of how other countries and terrorist groups view American power. For instance, one could argue that a war paradigm would result in more unilateral U.S. actions to counter terrorism, and that increased reliance on unilateral force might create tension with allies. Also, more frequent "acts of war" against terrorism may only embolden terrorists, and encourage an increasingly destructive action-reaction process.

Examining the full impact of the adoption of a war paradigm is beyond our scope here, and a recommendation for a war paradigm must be backed by further analysis. What we are proposing is that the USAF consider adopting some principles of the war paradigm in how it defends against and counters terrorism.

If we assume—and this is an uncertain assumption—that terrorist targets can be indisputably identified, then the USAF would be suited to key missions should the United States adopt a war paradigm. Air power offers a flexible, timely strike capability, including a new generation of highly discriminate weapons. It also affords the least politically risky of the military options for striking back at terror, because it does not entail putting troops on the ground or moving significant naval assets in harm's way. Moreover, the high speed of response associated with air power will become increasingly important as terrorists acquire the capabilities to move swiftly from one theater to another and to attack with little or no warning. Thus, the USAF, with the strike capabilities afforded by air-launched cruise missiles and other smart munitions, should be considered a natural, leading element in any proactive strategy for countering terror. Beyond direct bombardment, the USAF can provide tactical mobility for special forces teams—and give them close support—should they be called upon to strike directly at key terrorist nodes.

There are three fundamental ways in which air power could support a counterterrorist war paradigm. First, the USAF could play a major role in coercive diplomatic campaigns against state sponsors of terror, along the lines of the use of air power against Qaddafi in the 1986 air raid on Tripoli or the 1998 Tomahawk strikes in Sudan and Afghanistan.[92] Another possibility is that, instead of being used for

---

[92]Refer to Carr, 1996, and Hoffman and Carr, 1997, for a discussion of this issue.

coercive diplomacy, the USAF could be employed for either pre-emptive or preventive[93] strikes against terrorist or state-sponsored sites that foment terror (such as deep underground facilities where WMD might be produced). Finally, the USAF could be the key link, along with special forces, in an information war against the terrorists in terms of both striking at the key telecommunications nodes of terrorists, and gaining information about them via IW means.[94]

The last point merits some discussion. It is commonly argued that national technical means (NTM) of intelligence gathering are aimed at Cold War-era targets (i.e., tanks, planes, silos, etc.), and are therefore poorly suited to the needs of counterterrorism. This has led to calls for greater reliance upon human intelligence (humint) in dealing with terror. Humint is carried out by human operatives often working under cover or as double agents. Unfortunately, there are two principal limitations on the usefulness of humint regarding terrorists. First, organizations such as Hamas frequently recruit members when they are quite young, precluding infiltration of seasoned agents and making it more difficult to sway existing members or convince them to give up information. Second, advancing in a terrorist organization may require committing violent acts, including murder, which are incompatible with accepted Western intelligence practices. The source's reliability will always be in question, both in terms of the inherent risks of dealing with double agents and the likelihood that views expressed by the source are skewed by personal hatreds, rivalries, or mental instability. For these reasons, it is ill-advised to pin significant hopes on the development of sufficient humint sources to wage an effective counterterrorist campaign.

Instead, it may prove optimal to tailor NTM to the new needs of countering terror, relying less on satellite surveillance and perhaps rather more on drones and other pilotless craft capable of listening in

---

[93]Preemption refers to striking first in anticipation of an incipient attack. Prevention means striking before the opponent develops the capability to attack. For example, the Israeli Six Day War of 1967 was preemptive, in that the Israelis struck in anticipation of an attack. The Israeli air raid on Osirak in 1981 was preventive, because it was a strike to prevent Iraq from obtaining a nuclear capability.

[94]See John Arquilla, *From Troy to Entebbe: Special Operations in Ancient and Modern Times,* University Press of America, Lanham, Maryland, 1996, pp. 278–280.

on terrorists' increasingly advanced telecommunications. Coupling this with a joint IW capability for penetrating terrorist C2 nodes might well create a form of "virtual humint"[95] that will prove a key to counterterrorist strategy—and provide a new concept for the intelligence community. The approach will emphasize intelligence gathering by orbital assets or by human assets on the ground. But beyond the technological aspects of this form of counterterrorism, it will be crucial to rethink how to target terrorist groups. We next discuss how U.S. strategy might evolve.

Targeting Terrorists in the Information Age

The transition from hierarchical to networked terrorist groups is likely to be uneven and gradual. The netwar perspective suggests that, for the foreseeable future, various networked forms will emerge, coexisting with and influencing traditional organizations. Such organizational diversity implies the need for a counterterrorism strategy that recognizes the differences among organizational designs and seeks to target the weaknesses associated with each.

Counterleadership strategies or retaliation directed at state sponsors may be effective for groups led by a charismatic leader who enjoys the backing of sympathetic governments, but are likely to fail if used against an organization with multiple, dispersed leaders and private sources of funding. Networked organizations rely on information flows to function, and disruption of the flows cripples their ability to coordinate actions. It is no coincidence, for instance, that while the separation between Hamas political and military branches is well documented, this terrorist group jealously guards information on the connections and degree of coordination between the two.[96]

At the same time, the two-way nature of connectivity for information networks such as the Internet implies that the dangers posed by information warfare are often symmetric—the degree to which a terrorist organization uses information infrastructure for offensive purposes may determine its exposure to similar attacks by

---

[95]We are indebted to colleague Ian Lesser for this creative term.

[96]Bluma Zuckerbrot-Finkelstein, "A Guide to Hamas," *Internet Jewish Post,* available at *http://www.jewishpost.com/jewishpost/jp0203/jpn0303.htm.*

countering forces. While it is true that terrorist organizations will often enjoy the benefit of surprise, the IW tactics available to them can also be adopted by counterterrorists.

The key task for counterterrorism, then, is the identification of organizational and technological terrorist networks. Once such structures are identified, it may be possible to insert and disseminate false information, overload systems, misdirect message traffic, preclude access, and engage in other destructive and disruptive activities to hamper and prevent terrorist operations.

POLICY IMPLICATIONS AND CONCLUSIONS FOR THE USAF

The USAF can take various steps to effectively defend against and counter terrorism that is guided by a war paradigm. Defensive ideas and options might include:

1. *Do not modernize all communications nodes.* The USAF's C2 system is robust—it is designed to withstand the strains of protracted nuclear war—and full interconnectivity may in fact allow cyberterrorists to enter where they could not in the old C2 structure.

2. *Develop defensive antiterror standards for all operating bases and across mission types.* The standards should guarantee safety without constraining flexibility in varied settings; the standards may be more rigid in peacetime and in OOTW than in wartime.

3. *If terrorism worsens, increase reliance on CONUS basing and a wide network of dormant bases to reduce vulnerability of forward-based elements to a terrorist commando strategy.* While likely to make terrorism against USAF personnel and equipment more difficult, increased CONUS basing will be controversial because it entails military and political costs. First, general (i.e., ongoing peacetime) deterrence stability may suffer from the diminution of USAF presence abroad. With decreased deterrence there may be political fallout resulting from a dramatic withdrawal from key regions such as Europe. Third, terrorists might portray such redeployments as a "retreat" that they had caused, and a great victory over American power. Fourth, CONUS basing does not limit exposure to terrorist information warfare, and the risk of suffering delays in the "just in time" deployment process may increase. These downside factors

may be mitigated, however, by negotiating with friendly countries in key regions for access to bases that would be used only in times of crisis or for occasional engagement activities. Such an option would allow for prompt demonstration or deployment of USAF assets in crisis to shore up deterrence; and regular exercises in forward areas would show that USAF reach remains extensive and that terrorism has in no way forced a retreat. Finally, defense against terrorist information warfare would both enable and support CONUS basing.

For proactive counterterrorism, the USAF might consider the following:

4. *At the doctrinal level, consider development of a war paradigm to counter the activities of groups that see themselves as waging war against the United States.* This implies extending the list of what the USAF considers targets, to include more new-generation targets such as key nodes and the network itself. The adoption of a war paradigm may extend to the need for weapons designed to disrupt terrorist information flows, especially high-energy radio-frequency (HERF) and high-power microwave (HPM) weapons. The political and security implications of the adoption of such a paradigm would be profound, perhaps profoundly controversial—and need to be factored into future analyses.

5. *At the organizational level, deepen interservice and interagency networking.* The USAF is a principal actor in a counterterrorist war paradigm, and it should be a key node in an intergency network. As noted earlier, it may take networks to fight networks—and whoever masters the network form of organization will gain the greatest advantages.[97] Countering terror will require the formation of highly effective interagency and interservice mechanisms and command structures.

6. *In the intelligence realm, develop requirements for counterterrorist operations.* The USAF has a unique operating position in the area between orbital intelligence assets and humint, neither of which is likely to be effective against information-age terror. The Air Force might develop a form of "virtual humint" based on both hacking into

---

[97]See Arquilla and Ronfeldt, 1997; also, John Deutch, "Terrorism: Think Again," *Foreign Policy,* Fall 1997, pp. 10–20.

terrorist telecommunications nets and developing capabilities for reading "emanations" (communications read off of terrorist computer screens before they are encrypted). The latter capability would likely require use of very small unmanned aerial vehicles (UAVs) that are teleoperated by USAF information warfare personnel. In developing a capability of this sort, the Air Force would have to remain mindful of international legal constraints on such data "snooping."

7. *Continue planning for traditional operations such as raiding key terrorist nodes (in particular, deep underground [DUG] facilities that might produce weapons of mass destruction).* This, a key element of an eventual counterterrorist war paradigm, would require careful nodal analysis of terrorist groups to inform the campaign planning process.

The seven recommendations above are grouped according to their contribution to the four generic missions in Table 1.

These policy recommendations affect all the USAF missions, so that a balanced approach is achieved. A comprehensive counterterrorism policy ensures that the USAF can leverage its capabilities to the greatest extent while targeting the "soft spots" of information-age terrorist groups. However, the rise of networked terrorist organizations calls for a change in the analysis of terrorist groups. Analysts

Table 1

USAF Generic Counterterrorism Missions and Policy Recommendations

Mission	Recommendation
Political deterrence	Plan for traditional operations, with particular emphasis on DUG facilities.
Interdiction and strike	Develop weapons to attack network and information flows.
Intelligence gathering	Develop virtual humint capabilities with UAVs. Analyze nodes to identify networks. Form interagency networks.
Force protection	Switch to more CONUS basing and develop a network of dormant bases. Limit modernization of C2 nodes. Develop defensive counterterrorism standards.

should no longer assume that terrorist groups are bureaucratic, hierarchical, stand-alone organizations.

In closing, we note that the history of the 20th century has demonstrated the crucial importance of air power to the outcome of land and naval warfare. Now, with the coming of the information age, it may well be that the history of the 21st century will show that air power proved equally useful in determining the outcome of the struggle against terrorism.

Chapter Four

COUNTERING THE NEW TERRORISM: IMPLICATIONS FOR STRATEGY

Ian O. Lesser

INTRODUCTION

Terrorism is, among other things, a weapon used by the weak against the strong.[1] The United States will move into the 21st century as a preeminent, global power in a period of tremendous flux within societies, among nations, and across states and regions.[2] Terrorism will accompany changes at each of these levels, as it has in other periods of flux in the international environment. To the extent that the United States continues to be engaged as a global power, terrorism will have the potential to affect American interests directly and indirectly, from attacks on U.S. territory—including low-probability but

---

[1]This analysis deliberately avoids any detailed discussion of the definition of terrorism, in part because such discussions tend to be inconclusive but also because the rapidly changing nature of the phenomenon renders many traditional definitions misleading. The fashionable and often politically charged debate about terrorism makes the definition of terrorism a highly subjective, even ethno-centric exercise. The old adage about "one person's terrorist being another's freedom fighter" summarizes the problem. In RAND's continuing research on this subject, terrorism has generally been defined by the nature of the act, not the identity of the terrorists or the nature of the cause: "terrorism is violence or the threat of violence calculated to create an atmosphere of fear or alarm," generally in support of political or systemic objectives. See Karen Gardela and Bruce Hoffman, *RAND Chronologies of International Terrorism*, various years.

[2]The fact that we are approaching a new century and a new millennium may have implications in its own right for terrorism based on apocalyptic and messianic visions and for movements interested in "giving history a shove." See Walter Laqueur, "Fin-de-Siècle: Once More with Feeling," *Journal of Contemporary History*, Vol. 31, 1996, pp. 5–47.

high-consequence "superterrorism" with weapons of mass destruction—to attacks affecting our diplomatic and economic ties abroad, or our ability to maintain a forward military presence or project power in times of crisis. The United States will also have a unique, systemic interest in terrorism as a global problem—including acts of "domestic" terrorism confined within state borders that make up the bulk of terrorism worldwide—even where the United States is not directly or even indirectly targeted. In one way or another, terrorism can affect our freedom of action, not just with regard to national security strategy narrowly defined, but across a range of compelling issues, from drugs and money laundering to information and energy policy.

Many of our high-priority national objectives have been shaken by the recent experience of terrorism. The Oklahoma and World Trade Center bombings struck at our sense of security within our borders. Attacks against U.S. forces in Saudi Arabia raise questions about our strategy for presence and stability in an area of critical importance for world energy supply. The U.S. embassy bombings in Kenya and Tanzania raise questions about the exposure that comes with active engagement in world affairs, and point to the risks of privately sponsored terrorism. The assassination of Prime Minister Rabin and the campaign of suicide bombings in Israel has put the Middle East peace process in serious jeopardy, threatening a critical and longstanding U.S. diplomatic objective. Elsewhere, terrorism has destabilized allies (in Egypt and Turkey), and has rendered counternarcotics relationships difficult (in Colombia and Mexico). Where societies and regions are fundamentally unstable, and where political outcomes are delicately poised, terrorism will have a particular ability to affect strategic futures.

UNDERSTANDING AND COUNTERING THE "NEW" TERRORISM

This chapter explores the problem of terrorism in the broader national and international security context. It takes as its point of departure completed analyses of terrorism trends and prospects, as well as specialized assessments of weapons of mass destruction

(WMD) and information-related risks.[3] These analyses point to the steady augmentation of traditional patterns of terrorism by new forms of the phenomenon, both as stand-alone threats and in the context of more conventional conflict (i.e., as an asymmetric strategy). This new terrorism is increasingly networked; more diverse in terms of motivations, sponsorship, and security consequences; more global in reach; and more lethal. As a result, much existing counterterrorism experience may be losing its relevance as network forms of organization replace the canonical terrorist hierarchies, or as state sponsorship becomes more subtle and difficult to expose.

Similarly, many of the leading concepts of air power in relation to counterterrorism strategy may need to be revised. There will be a continuing need for preemption, deterrence, and retaliation in relation to state sponsors. But the key tasks for air and space power in the future may have as much or more to do with the surveillance, exposure, and targeting of nonstate actors, and even individuals. The transforming contribution of air and space power to national counterterrorism strategy will be making terrorism—an inherently amorphous phenomenon—more transparent for policymakers and the international community.

This chapter focuses to a great extent on "international terrorism" and terrorism in the international arena. The problem of domestic terrorism in the United States is addressed only in passing, a consequence of the need to limit the scope and focus of the study rather than a judgment about the significance of the problem. Indeed, the problem of domestic terrorism is growing and the threat of domestic and "insider" terrorism against U.S. military facilities and personnel would be a fertile area for further analysis. It is also worth noting that terrorism experts are increasingly uncomfortable with the traditional distinction between domestic and international terror in an age of global communications and networked terrorism.[4] Many of the most serious terrorist risks to U.S. national security—above all, those of

---

[3]See Chapters Two and Three.

[4]Confluence of the internal and external security environments, including terrorist risks, is especially striking in Europe with the weakening of borders and security problems linked to immigration. See Didier Bigo, "Security(s): Internal and External, the Mobius Ribbon," paper prepared for the International Studies Association, Toronto, March 18–22, 1997.

mass destruction and mass disruption in periods of crisis or conflict—can have a transnational dimension.

The following discussion places terrorism in strategic context by exploring terrorist threats to U.S. interests and future sources of risk, examines past U.S. and allied experience, offers a framework for counterterrorism strategy, and provides overall findings and implications for the U.S. military.

TERRORISM IN STRATEGIC CONTEXT

The Terrorist Threat to U.S. Interests: Four Dimensions

Terrorism provokes alarm and repugnance, but how meaningful is it as a threat to U.S. national security? Where does terrorism rank in relation to other security challenges? To gauge the extent of terrorism's challenge in strategic terms, it is useful to explore the terrorist threat to U.S. interests in four key dimensions: direct, indirect, systemic, and asymmetric. At the same time, perceptions and policies in relation to terrorism are being shaped by changing definitions of security and the evolving place of terrorism on the spectrum of domestic and international conflict.

Direct Threats

The most dramatic and proximate source of risk arises from direct terrorist attacks against U.S. citizens and property, overseas or on U.S. territory (or against U.S. forces in peacetime). The United States has been a leading target of international terrorists, a trend that shows few signs of abating.[5] Until recent years, however, few of these attacks took place within the United States, partly because traditional terrorist groups found the prospect of operations in the United States too difficult, politically counterproductive, or simply unnecessary. Most observers now believe the threshold for significant international terrorism in the United States has been crossed, especially in the wake of the World Trade Center bombing and the 1997 apprehension of terrorist bombers in New York. The prospect of further direct attacks within U.S. territory, coupled with

---

[5]See Chapter Two.

the increasing lethality of international terrorism, has begun to inspire new concerns about "homeland defense," above all defense against terrorist use of nuclear, biological, or chemical weapons against urban targets.

Regardless of changes in the size of the U.S. military presence abroad, there will always be more than enough U.S. citizens and interests engaged around the world (as businessmen, diplomats, students, and tourists) to provide ready targets for terrorists looking to strike at the United States. But the changing motivations and agendas of terrorists may raise the symbolic value of more-direct attacks against targets on U.S. territory. State sponsors, bent on revenge (e.g., Iraq or Libya), might see special merit in supporting operations within the United States. Similarly, movements with transcendental objectives, whether religious or political, may place greater emphasis on acts that shake the confidence and security of U.S. citizens at home. At the same time, the rise of terrorist networks blurs the distinction between domestic and international terrorism, and could facilitate the use of amateur proxies, including self-appointed proxies, for attacks within our borders.[6] Terrorist groups have already found the United States to be a fertile environment for fundraising and associated political activities. Some of this infrastructure could also be used to support more violent activities.

Terrorist motives for the direct attack of U.S. targets may be practical, systemic, or symbolic. In practical terms, terrorists may seek to alter U.S. policy or to influence public opinion with a specific objective (e.g., non-intervention in a regional conflict). In such cases, the use of force is likely to be limited and tailored to achieve a political end without an unintended backlash. Palestinian terrorism in the 1970s and 1980s fit this pattern, as did the attacks by Puerto Rican separatists in New York and at Muniz Air Base in 1981.[7] Unlike Western Europe, the United States has not suffered from pervasive "systemic"

---

[6]"Amateurs" along the lines of the conspirators involved in a July 1997 plot to bomb a Brooklyn, New York, subway station.

[7]The January 13, 1981, attack by a Puerto Rican terrorist group known as the Macheteros at Muniz Air National Guard base destroyed eight A-7 aircraft and damaged two others, causing some $45 million in damage. The same group claimed credit for a 1979 attack on a U.S. Navy bus. Jo Thomas, "Puerto Rico Group Says It Struck Jets," *New York Times*, January 13, 1981, p. 1.

terrorism, aimed at provoking fundamental social or political change. But the bombing in Oklahoma City as well as the militia movements suggest the existence of a reservoir of potential terrorism along these lines. Symbolic attacks, such as the bombing of Pan Am 107 or the World Trade Center bombing, imply fewer constraints on lethality and potentially much more destructive attacks. Without dismissing the potentially significant harm in terms of loss of life, economic disruption, and erosion of public confidence from direct attacks motivated by practical and systemic agendas, the strategic effect of such attacks is likely to be limited. Leading terrorism analysts tend to agree on the general ineffectiveness of terrorism as a weapon against well-established democracies, although some exceptions should be noted.[8] Certainly, there is little to indicate that terrorism or the threat of terrorism has been successful in changing U.S. policy on issues such as support for key allies or the use of force, much less questions of territorial integrity or domestic public policy. Similarly, the United States has not been a particularly fertile ground for ideological extremism of any stripe.

The Khobar Towers attack appears to have embraced both practical and symbolic motives—encouraging the departure of U.S. forces from Saudi Arabia, a blow to the Saudi regime, and, not least, a strike at U.S. power and prestige.[9] To the extent that the United States remains engaged as a strategic actor around the globe—or at least in key regions—the terrorist instrument is likely to remain as an attractive means of striking at far-flung manifestations of American power and influence, as well as host regimes (the symbolic component). It may also be an attractive tactic or strategy (if part of a campaign) to compel a U.S. withdrawal from specific regions or to severely limit the prospects for access, overflight, and security cooperation. The scale and value—in lives, money, and strategic utility—of the U.S. military overseas presence makes it an attractive target for terrorists motivated by practical and symbolic agendas.[10]

---

[8]Likely exceptions include the apparent success of IRA and Palestinian terrorism in compelling policy changes and gaining a seat at the political table.

[9]A sense of the various likely motivations of the Khobar Towers bombers can be found in a series of articles from the Arab press; see "The Saudi Bombing: Dissident Explains Why 'Indigenous' Groups May Do It Again," and "Why U.S. Forces Aren't Welcome in Saudi Arabia," *Mideast Mirror*, July 1 and 4, 1996.

[10]For a more detailed discussion, see Chapters Two and Three.

Symbolic terrorism of sufficient scale presents a different type of challenge. Certainly, terrorist use of weapons of mass destruction on U.S. soil, or against U.S. civilian or military targets abroad, would be a watershed event, especially if highly destructive. Concerns about the potential use of nuclear or other unconventional devices on U.S. soil—arguably higher now than during the nuclear targeting of the Cold War years—have become a significant feature of the national security debate.[11] Wider availability of WMD materials and expertise, coupled with the increasingly transcendental agendas of terrorist groups, are at the heart of this concern.[12] To the extent that terrorist use of WMD for symbolic purposes succeeds in significantly altering strategic thinking and perceptions of risk—as it almost certainly would—it might have a strategic effect by definition.

Certain types of terrorist campaigns aimed at the U.S. economy and information infrastructure could also impose significant costs.[13] The potential for information-based attacks on the banking, telecommunications, and electric-power systems is now widely debated. RAND analysis certainly suggests that terrorist networks are steadily acquiring the expertise to engage in such attacks, although their motivation to do so remains largely untested. Terrorists may well be more interested in "keeping the Net up" to use for their own intelligence and disinformation purposes.[14] Similarly, with the exception of hackers who acquire political agendas, terrorists are unlikely to engage in information warfare as an alternative to more destructive attacks. They are more likely to employ IW as a force multiplier—in combination with more conventional tactics—to avoid detection or to complicate efforts at mitigation and response. The progression from military and political targets to economic

---

[11]See, for example, Joseph S. Nye, Jr., and R. James Woolsey, "Defend Against the Shadow Enemy," *Los Angeles Times*, June 1, 1997, p. M5.

[12]See Robert H. Kupperman, "United States Becoming Target for Terror Forays," *National Defense*, January 1995.

[13]One variant might be a "dirty" conventional bomb—high-explosive combined with commercially available radiological material. Who would rent office space in a commercial center where such a device had been detonated, regardless of any cleanup? The result might be a potent weapon of economic denial in urban settings.

[14]See Chapter Three.

infrastructure—and potentially to information systems—has already been noted in relation to the evolution of IRA terrorism.[15]

Indirect Attacks Affecting U.S. Interests

Terrorist campaigns need not directly threaten U.S. lives and territory to affect American interests. Many U.S. allies, as well as key regional states, confront serious challenges arising from terrorism. Terrorism in Israel and the Palestinian territories is a potent spoiler in relation to the Middle East peace process—a key U.S. diplomatic interest—as well as threatening the stability of the West Bank and Gaza. PKK (Kurdistan Workers Party), Islamist, and leftist terrorism in Turkey affects the stability of a key NATO ally. Islamist violence in Egypt and elsewhere in the Middle East threatens the security of pro-U.S. regimes. The need to contain internal violence distorts the behavior of key actors, limiting their ability to play a positive regional role. Similar effects can be seen as a result of political and drug-related terrorism in Mexico, Colombia, and elsewhere in Latin America and the Caribbean.[16] Terrorism on America's southern periphery impedes political reform and, in many cases, prevents the development of bilateral cooperation on trade and investment. It can also be an important engine of uncontrolled migration and refugee movements affecting the United States.

Terrorism aimed at allied states can also have a more direct effect on U.S. citizens and interests, as witnessed through the 1970s and early 1980s in Western Europe and Japan. Acts carried out by groups such as the Red Brigades, the Bader-Meinhoff gang, Action Direct, November 17, and the Japanese Red Army Faction, aimed primarily at their own societies, occasionally spilled over into violence against American civilians and military personnel. Not only are terrorist risks becoming transnational, but with the growth of multinational businesses and nongovernmental organizations, the potential victims of terrorists are becoming less national and more global in character. Indeed, this has long been the case with international air

---

[15]Douglas Hayward, "Terrorists Target the Net," *TechWire* (Brussels), May 8, 1997.

[16]See Max G. Manwaring, "Security of the Western Hemisphere: International Terrorism and Organized Crime," *Strategic Forum*, No. 137, April 1998 (Institute for National Strategic Study, National Defense University).

travel; carriers may be national airlines, but the passengers are likely to be of varied nationality.

Systemic Consequences

A third perspective focuses on the overall consequences of terrorism, worldwide and domestic, for the international security environment and U.S. global engagement. The body of "international terrorist incidents," as defined by the leading terrorism databases, captures only a small fraction of global terrorism. Terrorist acts associated with international causes and Western targets claim the lion's share of media attention and policymakers' concern, but the vast bulk of terrorism worldwide is contained within state borders and is local in character. Factional terrorism in Algeria has probably claimed over 80,000 lives since 1992, and multiple incidents with as many as 100 deaths each continue to occur on a weekly basis. In Northern Ireland alone, deaths from domestic terrorism in some years have been four times the number of deaths from international terrorism in Europe as a whole.[17] If one includes the ethnic terrorism in sub-Saharan Africa, the Balkans, and the Caucasus, it becomes clear that terrorism's global toll in lives, property, and stability is larger indeed.

As a global power with global interests, the United States will be affected by instances of large-scale ethnic terrorism, even if the effects of this chaos—the breakdown of social and political order described by Robert Kaplan in terms of "the coming anarchy"—are distant and long term.[18] Mass terrorism in central Africa may be held at arm's length in Western perceptions. But even smaller-scale instances of ethnic terror in the Balkans, the Caucasus, or elsewhere in the former Soviet Union or China could significantly affect the strategic evolution of these regions. Third World and newly independent states are not only the major settings for terrorism, they are also the least well equipped in terms of resources and expertise to counter terrorist

---

[17]There were, for example, 62 in 1989. Paul Wilkinson, "Terrorist Targets and Tactics: New Risks to World Order," in Alison Jamieson (ed.), *Terrorism and Drug Trafficking in the 1990s*, Research Institute for the Study of Conflict and Terrorism, Aldershot, Dartmouth, UK, 1994, p. 9.

[18]Robert Kaplan, "The Coming Anarchy," *Atlantic Monthly*, Vol. 273, No. 2, February 1994, pp. 44–76.

challenges (although they may not feel the same constraints as liberal democracies in this context).[19]

Terrorism in the War Paradigm

Fourth, terrorism can take the form of an "asymmetric" strategy employed by adversaries in conflict with the United States or its allies, as a substitute for more conventional attacks, as a waypoint to more direct aggression, or as an adjunct to conventional warfare. This notion of terrorism in the "war paradigm"[20] is most likely to arise from the perception that the United States, and the West (including Israel) more generally, have developed an unassailable capacity for conventional warfare. As a result, regional competitors wishing to change the political or territorial order must contend with a perceived revolution in military affairs that has conferred disproportionate advantages on the most developed military powers. The experience of the Gulf War offers a key lesson in this regard. The Gulf War and subsequent operations in the Gulf, Bosnia, and elsewhere may also be seen as confirming the political will of the United States and its allies to use force in support of regional order.

A potential aggressor reviewing this experience may well draw the conclusion that terrorism (as well as other unconventional instruments such as the use of weapons of mass destruction) might be employed as a means of subverting regional competitors without necessarily triggering a U.S. response. Terrorism might provide a means of throwing deployed forces off balance, gaining time for the aggressor to consolidate a cross-border operation against a U.S. ally. Finally, it may also represent an attractive means of striking at the United States directly, for symbolism or revenge, and as a means of influencing U.S. public opinion when the costs and benefits of intervention are in debate. Some of these objectives might be achieved simply through the *threat* of terrorist attacks. The threat to use terrorists as a low-tech delivery system for chemical, biological, or nuclear weapons adds a troubling dimension.

---

[19]Wilkinson, "Terrorist Targets and Tactics," p. 9.

[20]I am grateful to RAND colleagues John Arquilla, David Ronfeldt, and Michele Zanini for this term (see Chapter Three).

That said, the systematic use of terrorism as a strategy by regional powers confronting the United States can face substantial obstacles, as the Iraqi experience during the Gulf War suggests. During the run-up to war in the Gulf, it was widely and reasonably predicted that Saddam Hussein would mobilize sympathetic terrorist organizations to engage in attacks on Western targets, both civilian and military.[21] In the event, terrorism was a negligible feature of the crisis, and Iraqi-sponsored terrorism certainly did not constitute anything like the potent "fifth column" some had envisioned. A range of explanations has been offered for the failure of Saddam Hussein's announced terrorism campaign, including pressure by other state sponsors (e.g., Syria), lack of planning and effective communications (exacerbated by the bombing campaign against Baghdad), and effective Western antiterrorism measures. The prospect for terrorist attacks against harder military targets in the Gulf was probably doubly limited by the short notice and the general unpreparedness of terrorist groups, especially those with close ties to Baghdad such as the Palestinian Liberation Front and the Fatah Revolutionary Council, for attacks on deployed forces.[22] With better preparation, both political and material, the outcome might have been quite different. Moreover, as discussed below, it may be too soon to gauge the longer-term effects of the Gulf War on Iraqi-sponsored terrorism.

A variation on this theme of terrorism as an asymmetric strategy goes further to suggest that unconventional modes of conflict will stem not just from the desire to outflank the United States but from a shift in the nature of conflict itself. In this paradigm, unconventional terrorist attacks on the sinews of modern, information-intensive societies will become the norm, largely replacing conventional conflicts over the control of territory or people. Carried to its logical conclusion, this is a future in which terrorism of all sorts, and especially information-related terrorism, becomes a more pervasive phenomenon, or even the dominant mode of war. It may, by definition,

---

[21]See, for example, Bruce Hoffman, *The Ultimate Fifth Column: Saddam Hussein, International Terrorism, and the Crisis in the Gulf*, RAND, P-7668, August 1990.

[22]These and other factors limiting Iraqi terrorism during the Gulf War are discussed in W. Andrew Terrill, "Saddam's Failed Counterstrike: Terrorism and the Gulf War," *Studies in Conflict and Terrorism*, Vol. 16, pp. 219–232.

have its greatest effect on the most highly developed economies, above all, the United States.[23]

Terrorism in various forms may be used deliberately by an adversary to deter certain types of attacks in war or during periods of tension in which U.S. intervention is likely. The use of air power, in particular, may face constraints imposed by mass hostage taking, including the dispersal of hostages to likely target sites. This tactic has been employed by Bosnian Serbs as a deterrent to NATO attacks, as well as by Saddam Hussein during the Gulf War and by Chechen separatists in their conflict with Moscow. This constraint can also be a factor in the more general problem of the discriminate use of air power in urban settings.

Changing Definitions of Security

A principal characteristic of terrorism, distinguishing it from many other forms of violence, is its ability to strike directly at perceptions of personal security. The potential for nuclear war or cross-border aggression by states may inspire a sense of fear among individuals, but the sense of vulnerability is collective and abstract. Individuals will certainly be the victims of conflict between states, but leaderships and military establishments are most often seen as the real targets.[24] By contrast, terrorism may be indiscriminate or precisely targeted, but in either instance the victims are individuals within society.

This characteristic of terrorism is arguably gaining visibility from the point of view of perpetrators and sponsors as well as publics and governments as post–Cold War definitions of security evolve. In addition to a greater emphasis on "economic security," "environmental security," and other issues that were of distinctly secondary importance during the Cold War, security perceptions are now increasingly driven by concerns about personal security and what

---

[23]A vision of radical change in the strategic environment along these lines is offered in Michael Vlahos, "The War After Byte City," *The Washington Quarterly*, Spring 1997.

[24]Even deliberate attempts to terrorize populations through strategic bombing are really aimed at weakening support for leaderships and military power.

may be termed "security of identity."[25] The terrorist instrument has particular leverage in both contexts. For example, the victory of Benjamin Netanyahu in the most recent Israeli elections was less the result of a referendum on the peace process than a referendum on personal security in the wake of multiple terrorist attacks. In many places around the world—including the United States—debates about security are to a great degree about personal security rather than the security of the state. This is certainly true in much of the Third World, and increasingly true in the former Soviet Union, where terrorism and crime are now rampant. One indicator of this phenomenon has been the rapid growth in private security services worldwide. This privatization of security may have some negative consequences for counterterrorism to the extent that more material and know-how finds it way into terrorist hands.

Security of identity has emerged as an important issue in many settings. It is not necessary to accept arguments about a global clash of civilizations to acknowledge that perceptions of cultural identity are shaping relations between societies and regions in the post–Cold War era. Violent reactions can arise when identities are under siege, sometimes in the form of terrorism. Current examples include the Uighur region in western China, Sri Lanka, Kashmir, and the Kurdish region of southeastern Turkey. Reactions to cultural assimilation can also take the form of global fears of cultural imperialism—a criticism most often aimed at the United States with its overwhelming role as purveyor of international tastes and information. The net result of this trend may be to increase the exposure of institutions engaged in integrative activities of all sorts (U.S. entertainment and communications firms, the European Union (EU) bureaucracies, regional organizations, etc.) to terrorist action.

Terrorism and the Conflict Spectrum

The canonical terrorist campaign in support of national liberation, religion, or ideology represents only a small portion of the ends to which terrorism is harnessed—and perhaps not even the most per-

---

[25]On security of identity, see, for example, Fernanda Faria and Alvaro Vasconcelos, "Security in North Africa: Ambiguity and Reality," *Chaillot Paper*, WEU (Western European Union) Institute for Security Studies, No. 25, September 1996, p. 5.

vasive. Terrorism occupies an increasingly broad place on the conflict spectrum, from activity barely distinguishable from crime or vendetta, through conventional terrorism in support of political and transcendental objectives, to potential "superterrorism," perhaps as a means of proxy war. The common denominator throughout is the use of terrorism as a tactic, an aspect in which terrorism is becoming more diverse. Indeed, the vocabulary of terrorism analysis reflects this diversity, with increasing reference to narco-terrorism, environmental terrorism, economic terrorism, info-terrorism, and other threats traditionally outside mainstream security concerns. Nor are these new dimensions of terror discrete points on the conflict spectrum. Rather, they may be difficult to differentiate at the margins and may reinforce one another. For example, the immense proceeds of drug trafficking can encourage narco-terrorism as a means of holding governments and rival cartels at bay, but may also increase the resources at the disposal of overtly political terrorist movements.[26] Similarly, there is growing suspicion that maritime piracy, an increasingly serious problem in many places around the world, is being carried out in some instances with state sponsorship. Terrorist movements are well placed to participate in such activities.[27]

To the extent that terrorist movements move toward network forms of organization and behavior, their ability to shift focus from one application of terrorism to another, or to pursue multiple applications simultaneously, will increase (as in the confluence of drug-related and political terror). Movements with political or religious agendas, but adept at applying similar tactics in other settings, may be recruited as proxies by state or nonstate sponsors looking to strike indirectly at U.S. or regional regimes. Terrorism's increasingly amorphous and diffuse nature has implications beyond the question of tactics and specific targets. Its diffusion is changing the nature of terrorism as a strategic problem.

---

[26]The Provisional IRA and, in particular, the PKK have come to rely extensively on drug smuggling as a source of support for politically motivated terrorism. See Jamieson, 1994.

[27]Libyan sponsorship is alleged in several instances of piracy and ship-disappearances off the North African coast. "Those in Peril on the Sea," *The Economist*, August 9, 1997, p. 40.

One consequence of the growing pervasiveness of terrorism as a tactic across the conflict spectrum is that counterterrorism may be less and less accurately portrayed as a stand-alone activity. Counterterrorism strategies are becoming a prominent feature of a range of public policies and national strategy objectives, from urban emergency preparedness and drug policy to regional security assistance and power projection.

Future Terrorism Geopolitics

Terrorism and counterterrorism have most often been seen through a regional lens, with a natural focus on key regions such as the Middle East where terrorism has been pervasive and capable of reshaping political and strategic futures. Domestic terrorism, especially in the Third World, has been relatively neglected despite the enormous volume of incidents. Most recently, it has become fashionable to look beyond domestic and regional terrorism to consider transnational or global challenges. As other parts of this analysis suggest, there is good reason to take various transnational risks more seriously given the increasingly free movement of people and information, and the rise of networks based on these trends.

Despite these factors, it is arguable that the bulk of terrorism of whatever sort, worldwide, will have national or regional sources, even if terrorist activity crosses state and regional divides. True network terrorism may arise, where grievances and activists exist without reference to geography but are based solely on shared, functional agendas. Single-issue ideological or religious movements already exhibit some of these qualities. Yet much terrorism touching on U.S. interests will have an identifiable source, whether functional or geographic, with implications for counterterrorism strategy and planning.

Ethnic Separatism and Frustrated Nationalism. The post-1945 decolonization struggles brought a wave of terrorist campaigns affecting North and sub-Saharan Africa, South and Southeast Asia, and the Middle East, as well as the territories of the colonial powers themselves. In some cases, such as Algeria, the scale of terrorist violence associated with this period has left an enduring legacy. The post-Soviet, post–Cold War environment has encouraged a new wave of ethno-nationalist violence and much outright terrorism. In recent years, terrorism has been an instrument of large-scale "ethnic cleansing" in the Balkans, the Caucasus, and central Africa. The impetus to create new states out of nations, and at a minimum, to carve out greater autonomy for ethnic groups, seems likely to persist as a key feature of the post–Cold War world.[28] As in the 1940s, 1950s, and 1960s, terrorism is likely to be an accompanying feature of ethnic and national assertiveness. In particular, terrorism is likely to be most prominent as a catalyst in the early stages of ethnic conflict, "as a violent prelude to state formation," and in later stages as an expression of frustration or revenge in ethnic and nationalist endgames.[29]   Where insurgent movements have adopted terrorist tactics, this use of terrorism could increase as movements are defeated or contained.[30]

For every separatist movement that succeeds, many are likely to be unsuccessful, and the resulting frustration and perhaps desire for revenge against central authorities and intervening powers may be strong. The increasing incidence of terrorist attacks against SFOR (the UN Stabilization Force) in Bosnia and the persistence of Chechen attacks against Russian targets even in the wake of a settlement provide useful examples.[31] This phenomenon may also be present in the Middle East, where few would now disagree that a Palestinian state is inevitable. Yet the contours of the Palestinian-Israeli end-game are being defined by terrorism, despite the apparent success of the decades-long Palestinian drive for self-determination. In other cases—the Basque Homeland and Freedom movement, known by its Basque initials as ETA, in Spain and the Provisional IRA in Northern Ireland are exemplars—the political situation may evolve sufficiently to make the original terrorist cause

---

[28]See Graham E. Fuller, "Redrawing the World's Borders," *World Policy Journal*, Vol. 14, No. 1, Spring 1997.

[29]James Der Derian, *Antidiplomacy: Spies, Terror, Speed, and War*, Blackwell, Cambridge, 1992, p. 105. For a discussion of the various roles of ethnic terrorism, see Daniel Byman, "The Logic of Ethnic Terrorism," unpublished paper prepared for the Council on Foreign Relations roundtable on terrorism, April 1997.

[30]Brian Michael Jenkins, *Future Trends in International Terrorism*, RAND, P-7176, 1985, p. 8.

[31]Recent terrorist threats against U.S. targets in Albania, and the August 1998 bombing of the U.S. Information Center in Kosovo, provide further examples.

an anachronism.[32]   But the tradition and infrastructure of terror remain and pose a continuing residual threat to security.

Looking ahead, the successor states of the former Soviet Union represent a reservoir of ethno-nationalist terrorism. Unlike other such reservoirs in sub-Saharan Africa and Latin America, political violence emanating from these countries has a higher potential to affect U.S. interests given the region's energy reserves, the presence of nuclear weapons, and the general significance of Russian futures for international security.

Religious Extremism and "Postmodern" Terrorism. The rise of religious terrorist movements over the past two decades is significant in several respects. First, it represents a significant shift away from the measured political agendas associated with ideological and national liberation groups active in the 1960s and 1970s.[33] Second, and partly as a result of its transcendental or "total" character, it has been responsible for much of the increase in terrorism's lethality over the past decade. Third, religious terrorism is in no sense limited to Islamic extremists. Terrorism has been a favored tactic for violent confrontations across religious faultlines within and between states, whether in Kashmir, the former Yugoslavia, Egypt, or Sudan. Among Palestinians, Bosnians, Chechens, Sikhs, and others, politicized religious movements have played a key role in the evolution of political violence and have emerged as a geopolitical force.[34] There is little evidence that terrorism is losing its salience in this setting.

The approach of the millennium has significance for a variety of religious and transcendental groups. The result could be an even more potent tendency toward nihilist and transcendental violence which has accompanied the end of previous centuries. Extremist millenarians and other groups on the pattern of the Aum Shinrikyo (Supreme

---

[32]See Marlise Simons, "Spain Turns on Rebels with Outrage," *New York Times*, July 18, 1997.

[33]For an excellent discussion of the characteristics of religious terrorism, see Bruce Hoffman, *Holy Terror: The Implications of Terrorism Motivated by a Religious Imperative*, RAND, P-7834, 1993.

[34]See Magnus Ranstorp, "Terrorism in the Name of Religion," *Journal of International Affairs*, Vol. 50, No. 1, Summer 1996; and Mark Juergensmeyer, "The Worldwide Rise of Religious Nationalism," *Journal of International Affairs*, Vol. 50, No. 1, Summer 1996.

Truth) cult in Japan may well wish to "give history a shove" through acts of superterrorism with weapons of mass destruction, and U.S. and other Western societies generally may offer especially symbolic targets. Such groups may also be among the most likely to envision transnational acts of destruction and disruption. In this context, it is notable that by 1995 the Aum cult responsible for the lethal sarin gas attack on the Tokyo subway had more members in Russia than in Japan.[35] Groups motivated by apocalyptic impulses, together with the maturing of more traditional politically oriented terrorist movements, suggest the rise of what Walter Laqueur has described as "postmodern terrorism."[36]

Low-Intensity Product of Regional Rivalries. The post–Cold War world abounds in active state-to-state rivalries, largely along south-south rather than north-south lines. Some rivalries will result in conventional threats to borders and direct confrontations between regimes. In other cases, the costs of direct confrontation may be too high or outcomes too uncertain. Those states may wish to exert pressure through other means, including terrorism, most likely carried out through proxies. Current examples include North Korean sponsorship of terrorism against South Korea; Syrian and Iranian support for PKK terrorism in Turkey; Sudanese and Iranian support for Islamist terrorism in Egypt and other Middle Eastern states; and Pakistani sponsorship of Kashmiri terrorism in India. A revived Iraq with regional ambitions might well turn to the terrorism instrument as a lever in dealing with neighboring regimes. In Europe, the potential for Western intervention in Balkan rivalries may fuel less-direct attempts at pressure and subversion through terrorism.[37] Alleged Greek support for the PKK could, if relations deteriorate

---

[35]Walter Laqueur, "Fin-de-Siècle: Once More with Feeling," *Journal of Contemporary History*, Vol. 31, 1996, p. 38.

[36]See Walter Laqueur, "Postmodern Terrorism," *Foreign Affairs*, Vol. 75, No. 5, September–October 1996.

[37]This would mark a return to traditional patterns of political violence in the Balkans. Prior to World War I, Serb and Macedonian nationalism were virtual bywords for terrorism. Some of the most violent groups active in that period still exist, including IMRO (Internal Macedonian Revolutionary Organization).

in the Aegean, lead to an escalating tit-for-tat campaign of state-sponsored terrorism.[38]

New Ideological Clashes. In the wake of the collapse of the Soviet Union, the notion of ideological struggle disappeared from the strategic scene. Those regimes still professing a socialist or communist agenda—Cuba, North Korea, China (in a formal sense)—appeared as quaint anachronisms. In the realm of terrorism, few vigorous movements remain on the extreme left. Some, such as the Shining Path and Tupac Amaru movements in Peru have suffered striking defeats in recent years. In Italy, Germany, France, and elsewhere in Europe, leftist and anarchist terror has been effectively contained since the early 1980s.[39]

Has this apparent triumph of liberal capitalism entirely undercut the ideological bases for 20th-century terror? The outlook in terms of political violence is not as clear as speculations about the "end of history" might suggest. Indeed, it is possible that the apparent victory of liberal democracy in the Cold War also contains the seeds of a reaction, perhaps of violence. Economic transformation and reform across the former communist bloc is producing uneven results and is engendering resentment in many quarters. Even in the West, the dismantling of the welfare state, especially in Europe, is having a divisive effect on societies with high rates of unemployment. Elsewhere, economic reform and higher rates of economic growth are producing marked disparities in income and a mounting perception of inequality. In countries such as Mexico, Turkey, Egypt, and Indonesia, the divide between "haves" and "have nots" is making issues of class and economic opportunity central to political change. Given past experience in societies as diverse as 19th century Russia and 20th century Iran, it would be surprising if some portion of frustration with economic conditions did not find expression in acts of

---

[38]Perception may be as important as reality in this regard. Turkish claims of a Greek role here remain difficult to substantiate beyond the open political support of the PKK by some Greek politicians.

[39]Greece and Turkey still face minor terrorist risks from this quarter: Dev-Sol and Dev-Yol in Turkey (the PKK also professes a leftist ideology); and November 17 in Greece.

terrorism. Anarchism and communitarianism may yet reemerge as sources of terrorist violence in the 21st century.[40]

However, the connection among economic deprivation, political frustration, and terrorism is not clear or direct. Contemporary research has not been able to demonstrate any clear-cut relationship "between poverty, scarcity, inflation, or any other socioeconomic indicator and terrorism. Indeed, countries experiencing the highest levels of terrorism are often among the economically and socially most advanced nations in their region, and often the least authoritarian."[41] As with other forms of political turmoil and violence, relative rather than absolute deprivation may be a more significant influence on the rise of terrorism.

Extreme right-wing terrorism existed alongside the more prominent leftist groups of the 1970s and early 1980s, and was responsible for highly lethal attacks, especially in Italy and Turkey. In the 1990s, right-wing extremism emerged as a violent force in Germany, Austria, and elsewhere in Europe. Attacks against immigrants and "foreigners" have been at the heart of these movements, but given their nationalist character, it is not inconceivable that U.S. military forces and civilians in Europe could emerge as targets. In the United States, right-wing militia and survivalist movements are a prominent source of terrorist risk, and are increasingly networked with like-minded groups worldwide. In short, ideologically motivated terrorism in the developed world is now as likely to emerge from the right as from the left.

Another potential source of terrorism might arise from the evolution of international relations along the conflictual, "civilizational" lines suggested by Samuel Huntington.[42] At their most ragged, these civilizational frictions could have terrorism as a central feature, both within societies (especially the "torn" societies in Huntington's model) and among states—or like-minded groupings of states, par-

---

[40]At least one observer identifies a totalitarian impulse in modern terrorism. See Fred Charles Iklé, "The Second Coming of the Nuclear Age," *Foreign Affairs*, Vol. 75, No. 1, 1996, pp. 119–128.

[41]Jenkins, 1985, p. 6.

[42]See Samuel P. Huntington, *The Clash of Civilizations and the Remaking of World Order*, Simon and Schuster, New York, 1996.

ticularly where conventional military confrontations are deterred or impractical. Among current terrorist movements, the extremist transnational Islamic groups (e.g., the Arab Afghans) come closest to this model. Taking the Huntingtonian approach to extremes, one might speculate about the possibility of terrorist groups acting against the United States with Chinese sponsorship sometime in the 21st century, against the background of a U.S.–China cold war. A revived and antagonistic Russia could also emerge as the sponsor of terrorist proxies acting against U.S. interests and impelled by nationalist rather than leftist ideology. More likely, official and intellectual criticism in Asia and elsewhere of Western cultural dominance could encourage extremists, perhaps beyond the control of governments, to carry this critique into the terrorist realm.

Crime, Drugs, and the Privatization of Security—and Terror. Transnational crime, much of it related to drug trafficking, has emerged as a leading source of violence within both developed and developing societies.[43] The weight of this criminal activity in many economies encourages the spillover of criminal violence into the political realm. States in Latin America and elsewhere are becoming destabilized through narco-terrorism. In Italy, the war between organized crime (the Mafia, Ndraghetta, and Camora) and the state has at times spilled over into acts of outright terrorism.[44] In Turkey, proceeds from the drug trade have been used to support PKK terrorism as well as the counterterrorist activities of right-wing nationalist groups.

Colombia provides the most striking contemporary example of this problem and its bearing on U.S. interests. There, private paramilitary armies exist alongside the Colombian military, violent drug cartels, and left-wing insurgents. Terrorist tactics have become the norm in relations among these groups, and Colombia now faces the dismal prospect of deterioration into a narco-state or outright disintegration.[45] Colombian terrorism is also beginning to undermine

---

[43]Bruce Hoffman identifies crime as a clear trend, especially in Colombia and Peru, where drug cartels have developed close links with terrorist and guerrilla organizations. Hoffman, 1998, pp. 27–28.

[44]For example, the May 1993 bombing of the Uffizi Gallery in Florence, Italy.

[45]James L. Zackrison and Eileen Bradley, "Colombian Sovereignty under Siege," *Strategic Forum*, National Defense University, Washington, DC, May 1997.

regional stability, with particular effect on the border with Venezuela.[46] One consequence of this situation has been Colombia's emergence as a leading source of international and specifically anti-U.S. terrorism—Colombia led the global tally of anti-U.S. incidents with 56 in 1995 and 53 in 1996.[47]

As the United States becomes more heavily involved in counternarcotics cooperation with Mexico, Peru, Panama, Venezuela, Ecuador, and Brazil—and possibly, Colombia—the potential for narco-terrorism against U.S. targets, civilian and military, will likely increase. Any proposals for expanded assistance, including air interdiction, will raise new force protection problems for U.S. forces deployed to the region.[48] In an era of transnational terrorist networks (and drug cartels have been at the forefront of such networking), it is possible for narco-terrorists to strike for practical or symbolic reasons at U.S. targets far from the area of operations in Latin America and the Caribbean.

The spread of transnational violence associated with international criminal activity is also one of the elements fueling rapid growth in the private security field worldwide. Multinational corporations, nongovernmental aid organizations, and others exposed to criminal and politically motivated terrorism are increasingly reliant on the services of security firms, which now must be considered antiterrorism actors in their own right, alongside states and international organizations. This trend is particularly pronounced in Latin America, Africa, and the former Soviet Union, where crime and terrorism—often the two are difficult to distinguish—have become leading challenges for foreign businesses and investors. Yet this privatization of security also raises the prospect of growing security information and expertise on the international market and thus potentially at the service of terrorist networks.

The interaction between transnational criminal organizations and political terrorism raises special concerns. This interaction is in no

---

[46]See "Cross-Border Terror," *The Economist*, May 24, 1997, p. 70.

[47]Department of State Regional Terrorism Overview, 1995–1996.

[48]See Clifford Krauss, "Pentagon to Help Peru Stop Drug-Base Shipping on Rivers," *New York Times*, February 3, 1997.

sense new, and terrorist organizations as diverse as Shining Path in Peru and the PKK in Turkey derive substantial revenue from drug-related commerce. But the enormous sums of money involved, as well as numerous points of contact between leading mafias and legitimate institutions, can facilitate acts that would be difficult for politically motivated terrorist groups to undertake—and pay for—on their own. This is a particular risk in relation to nuclear terrorism. Although details remain murky, Russian mafias are already reported to be involved in obtaining and smuggling nuclear materials, and in the most extreme case, perhaps even small nuclear weapons.[49] Further turmoil in Russia could worsen the outlook for control of nuclear materials and technology. As the conflict between transnational mafias and concerned states becomes more direct, it raises the possibility that mafias themselves will threaten nuclear or other forms of unconventional terrorism.

As the experience with Osama bin Laden, a rogue Saudi businessman with extreme Islamist and anti-American views, suggests, the future environment may see more international terrorism financed by private means. Private sponsors of terrorist movements, not necessarily limited to Islamic radicalism and with full access to information technologies and techniques, may find it convenient to operate against regimes, rival movements, or the United States from far-flung bases. And as the bin Laden experience shows, targets will include the relatively "hard" U.S. overseas military presence as well as softer diplomatic and civilian targets.[50] Bin Laden established himself in Afghanistan, along with other Arab Afghans, and Sudan offers another congenial environment. In the future, bases for privately sponsored terrorism might as easily be found in unstable regions elsewhere—in the Balkans or the Caucasus, or where wealthy elites exist against a background of strong anti-Western resentment, such as Malaysia. Arguably, the decline in overt state sponsorship may

---

[49]Douglas Farah, "Freeh Says Russian Mafias Pose Growing Threat to U.S.: FBI Chief Also Warns of Nuclear Banditry," *Washington Post*, October 2, 1997.

[50]After the Khobar Towers bombing, bin Laden issued explicit calls for a holy war against U.S. forces in the Gulf. Robert Fisk, "Saudi Calls for Jihad Against U.S. 'Crusader'," *The Independent*, September 2, 1996; and report interview with bin Laden in Afghanistan, *The Independent*, July 10, 1996. The full text of the declaration was published in *Al-Islah* (London), FBIS-NES-96-173, September 2, 1996.

stimulate the rise of privately sponsored terrorism—the dark side of global philanthropy.

Losers in Confrontations with the United States and the West. Losers in confrontations with the United States may turn to terrorism as a means of expressing their frustration or carrying on their armed struggle. Such attacks may be launched against targets within the United States, or aimed at U.S. citizens or interests abroad. They may be carried out by aggrieved states, or conducted by networks of sympathetic individuals, including diaspora groups, with or without the knowledge and backing of state actors. In the wake of the Gulf War, Baghdad apparently sanctioned a failed attempt to assassinate former President Bush, and some analysts have alleged an Iraqi hand in both the World Trade Center bombing and the 1995–1996 bombing against U.S. military targets in Saudi Arabia.[51] Given the scale of the military defeat and subsequent economic devastation inflicted on Iraq, it would be surprising if the United States did not continue to confront a risk of Iraqi-supported terrorism motivated largely by revenge and the desire to burnish Iraq's image in radical circles. Similarly, Iranian support for terrorism against U.S. targets in the Gulf and elsewhere may be aimed, in part, at keeping the United States off balance. A good deal of the impetus, however, may come from a less rational desire for revenge against the U.S. policy of isolation and containment.

There will be other, future candidates for sponsorship of revenge-based terrorist campaigns against the United States and its allies, including radical Serb nationalists angered at NATO's role in Bosnia or Mexican drug lords enraged by aggressive U.S. antidrug efforts. Moreover, terrorist campaigns based in deep-rooted anger over defeat or abuses, real or perceived, can be very long-lived, as the almost hundred-year history of Armenian revenge attacks on Turkish officials demonstrates.

It is worth asking why this form of terrorism looms as a serious risk in today's environment, when it did not follow the defeat of major powers in two world wars. The difference may lie in the fact that the Gulf War, the U.S. engagement in Bosnia, and the cold war with Iran all

---

[51]See Laurie Mylroie, "The World Trade Center Bomb: Who is Ramzi Yousef? And Why It Matters," *The National Interest*, Winter 1995–1996.

involve disproportionate power relationships. In addition, the propensity for terrorism on the part of the defeated or "contained" may be influenced by the extent of their isolation from the international community. Under certain conditions, as in the case of Iraq, there may be strategic reasons for maintaining a policy of post-defeat containment, even if the risk of revenge-based terrorism is increased. Another possible explanation is that the rules of the game have changed, with states now more willing to engage in terrorism as an expression of frustration in their relations with stronger powers (would a defeated France have engaged in state-sponsored terrorism against Germany in the wake of the Franco-Prussian War?). Yet another useful distinction may be made between status quo and revolutionary states, with the former generally reluctant to use terrorism as an instrument of revenge, even in defeat or political frustration.

Anarchy and Rage. Western views of terrorism have been shaped by the period of nationalist and ideological terrorism, and more recently by the challenge of religious and "postmodern" terrorism. As a result, analysts and policymakers are attuned to the question of terrorist agendas, whether political or transcendental. Yet a considerable amount of global terrorism defies this sort of explanation. The horrific violence in Algeria springs from a political crisis, but is increasingly divorced from any coherent political explanation. What began as a struggle between the military government and extremists bent on the establishment of an Islamic state has deteriorated into a shadowy war of all against all, in which personal and clan vendettas, factional struggles, and criminal infighting probably account for much of the "terrorist" violence. Despite the government's claims to have contained the terrorism, the country hovers on the verge of anarchy. The most clearly discernible impetus behind the violence is the profound alienation—rage is perhaps the more accurate term— of younger Algerians with no economic or social prospects.

Terrorism in Algeria is a striking case of a phenomenon also seen elsewhere. Arguably, Rwanda, Haiti, and Somalia provide other examples where political crises have given way to terrorist behavior and popular rage, often divorced from any clear political agenda.[52]

---

[52]The violence accompanying the partition of India and Pakistan after independence had some of the same hallmarks.

The net result is a dissolution of society and normal constraints on violence. In the worst case, this is the future foreseen by some observers for the 21st century's failed states. Populations are terrorized, and this terror may spill over to affect adjacent or involved states (as in the case of Algeria and France), but much of the original motivation for terrorism and counterterrorism has evaporated. Levels of underdevelopment and social stress in Africa, Latin America, and parts of Asia suggest that there is a reservoir of terrorism flowing from anarchy and rage. Much of this violence may not resemble terrorism in the classical sense, but the challenges it poses for Western policymakers and security establishments may be very similar, especially where foreigners emerge as favored targets.

Implications for the Future

Our discussion of future sources of terrorism contains implications for counterterrorism strategy and planning, most notably:

- The United States will need to look beyond traditional agendas and traditional regions in anticipating terrorist risks. Over the next decade, the Balkans, the Caucasus, and other centers of ethnic conflict could well emerge as leading producers and exporters of terrorism affecting U.S. interests.

- To a far greater extent than in the past, both terrorists and their victims may have little to do with states and much more to do with nonstate—even private or criminal—concerns.

- The revolution in military affairs may drive less-capable powers (i.e., most of the actors in the international system) toward asymmetric strategies when in conflict with the United States and its allies, and these strategies may well include conventional and unconventional terrorism.

- New ideological struggles may emerge to fuel terrorism aimed at the security of individuals, states, and the international system itself.

- Successful U.S. engagement in the management or shaping of the security environment in key regions may produce residual risks in the form of terrorism carried out by the defeated or contained.

- Finally, there may be a growing tendency toward terrorism divorced from any coherent political agenda, motivated instead by transcendental or nihilist objectives, or simply rage at the failure of some societies and the success of others.

To the extent that most terrorism, worldwide, will remain within the borders of affected societies and will not have the United States as an explicit target, the phenomenon will have highly variable consequences for U.S. security. We must recognize that U.S. exposure goes beyond the direct vulnerability of citizens, property, and territory. Terrorism also has the potential to affect U.S. interests indirectly but significantly—through attacks on allies, corrosive effects on the stability of key states and regions, as well as broader, systemic consequences for the international security environment.

THE LESSONS AND RELEVANCE OF COUNTERTERRORISM EXPERIENCE

U.S. Experience: A Mixed Legacy

The U.S. counterterrorism experience yields ambiguous lessons for analysts, policymakers, and military planners. Unlike many of our allies, we have not until recently faced a real domestic terrorist threat. Over the past decades, the United States has been a prominent target internationally while enjoying virtual sanctuary within its borders. U.S. security interests have been threatened by terrorism, both directly and indirectly, but the stability and survival of the U.S. as a society has never been seriously threatened by terrorism—and is unlikely to be. In these respects, the U.S. experience is sharply differentiated from that of other key states where international terrorism has been a prominent, even existential concern.

A full survey of the evolution of U.S. counterterrorism policy is beyond the scope of this discussion, but it is worth touching on some of the key, enduring facets.[53] The most visible and controversial elements of U.S. counterterrorism policy have involved the use of force,

---

[53]A good recent survey of the role of various U.S. agencies in implementing counterterrorism policy can be found in *Combating Terrorism: Federal Agencies' Efforts to Implement National Policy and Strategy*, General Accounting Office, GAO/NSIAD-97-254, Washington, DC, September 1997.

including air power in various forms—a pattern already evident in the global debate over the U.S. cruise missile strikes against terrorism-related targets in Afghanistan and Sudan. Indeed, there is a long experience along these lines. Apart from the ordeal of the U.S. embassy hostage crisis in Tehran and the failed attempt at intervention, the leading image of U.S. counterterrorism policy is the 1986 Operation El Dorado Canyon against Libya, ordered in response to Libyan involvement in the bombing of a Berlin disco frequented by U.S. military personnel. The air strike and its effects have been heavily debated. With the exception of Britain, allied support for the operation was poor, and many observers interpreted the operation as an unsuccessful effort to assassinate Colonel Qaddafi. Arguably, the operation was designed to send a broad political signal, reduce Libyan enthusiasm for the sponsorship of international terrorism, and demonstrate a U.S. willingness to act. The last motivation, while more vague in intent, should not be underestimated. Indeed, the desire for strategic catharsis is arguably an important component of counterterrorism policy generally.

The Libyan case yields ambiguous lessons. On the one hand, the widespread perception that Operation El Dorado Canyon dissuaded the Libyan regime from further acts of terror does not withstand close scrutiny. After a brief respite, Libya appears to have resumed, even increased, its involvement in international terrorism. At least 15 incidents in 1987 and eight in 1988 have been linked to Libya. The 1988 bombing of Pan Am 103 in which 278 died is the most dramatic example of terrorism with a Libyan connection in the wake of the 1986 confrontation. Libyan-sponsored terrorism aimed at Britain (including new support for the IRA) also gathered pace after 1986.[54]

On the other hand, it is difficult to measure the deterrent effect on Libyan behavior in net terms. Even more ambitious terrorist campaigns may have been planned and interrupted. The need for more covert sponsorship may well have reduced the scope of support and the scale of incidents in the years following Operation El Dorado Canyon. The deterrent effect of the air strike on other state sponsors

---

[54]Libya's terror campaign in this period included attempts at operations within the United States itself (e.g., the recruitment of a Japanese Red Army terrorist, Yu Kikumura, for a planned bombing in the Wall Street area). See the RAND-St. Andrews Chronology of International Terrorism and the discussion in Chapter Two.

of terrorism is similarly difficult to measure. Overall, narrow measures of the utility of military responses to international terrorism (How many incidents prior? How many incidents after?) may not be the most appropriate for a global power with systemic interests in the containment of terrorism and the maintenance of credibility in security terms. Having established Libyan culpability, especially against the background of a broader U.S.-Libyan confrontation, some direct response was inevitable and required.

Before the events of August 1998, less attention had been devoted to U.S. operations aimed at individuals implicated in terrorist acts against U.S. citizens. Examples include the 1987 capture of Fawaz Younis, a Lebanese terrorist aboard a yacht near Cyprus and his subsequent trial and imprisonment in the United States; the interception of an Egyptian aircraft carrying terrorists involved in the *Achille Lauro* hijacking and their seizure at Sigonella; and the capture in Pakistan of Mir Aimal Kansi, responsible for the 1993 shooting outside the CIA headquarters in Virginia. The strikes against the bin Laden infrastructure in Afghanistan provide a more recent example. Indeed, these more personalized applications of surveillance and the use of limited force may become prominent features of future policy to counter the new terrorism.

The thrust of U.S. counterterrorism policy has been the application of economic sanctions against state sponsors, multilaterally where possible, and domestic legislation.[55] The Omnibus Terrorism Act of 1986 made terrorist attacks on U.S. citizens abroad a federal crime and authorized extraterritorial arrest and trial in U.S. courts. Counterterrorism legislation developed under the Clinton Administration reflects the changing nature of terrorism and focuses on transnational threats, weapons of mass destruction, and terrorist funding sources. Like many of its allies, the United States has been committed in principle to the policy of "no negotiations" with terrorists, but this policy has been overwhelmed on numerous occasions by the pressure for resolution. Negotiations were integral to the release of the hostages in Teheran, and the United States has negoti-

---

[55]The current list of state sponsors subject to varying sanctions includes Libya, Iran, Iraq, Cuba, North Korea, Syria, and Sudan.

ated officially and unofficially for the release of hostages in Lebanon, including the notorious arms-for-hostages deal with Iran.[56]

In the post–Cold War period, there has been a refocus of intelligence collection and analysis on terrorist risks, among other unconventional security challenges. Finally, there is a tradition of hardening in response to terrorist risks. The first wave of hardening came as a response to the hijackings of international airliners in 1970s and 1980s, often with loss of American lives. The current worldwide system of airport security has its origins in this era, and the United States remains a strong advocate for further hardening of air travel. Most analysts would judge efforts in this area to have been quite successful in reducing the incidence of hijackings and attacks on commercial aircraft.[57] A second period of hardening is now under way as a result of the Khobar Towers bombing, the embassy bombings in Tanzania and Kenya, and the perception of a growing terrorist threat to the U.S. military and civilian presence overseas.

Just as terrorism is becoming an overtly transnational problem, the international dimension of counterterrorism policy is acquiring greater importance, both in terms of cooperative efforts and of comparative lessons to be learned. With this in mind, it is useful to explore perceptions and lessons from the experience of three key allies—Britain, France, and Israel.[58] Although each has faced quite different terrorism risks, and the exposure of all three differs in important respects from that of the United States, aspects of their experience and counterterrorism strategies are relevant to the U.S. debate. In particular, these countries have their own understanding of national vulnerability, force protection problems, and the changing nature of terrorism. They also have distinct views about American exposure and policy with regard to international terrorism. Like the

---

[56]On the evolution of U.S. policy through the late early 1990s, see J. Brent Wilson, "The United States' Response to International Terrorism," in David A. Charters (ed.), *The Deadly Sin of Terrorism: Its Effect on Democracy and Civil Liberty in Six Countries,* Greenwood, Westport, Connecticut, 1994.

[57]See Paul Wilkinson, "Airline Security," unpublished paper, University of St. Andrews, Scotland, 1997.

[58]A good comparative and analytical survey of a wider set of counterterrorism experiences can be found in Bruce Hoffman and Jennifer Morrison Taw, *A Strategic Framework for Countering Terrorism and Insurgency,* RAND, N-3506-DOS, 1992.

United States, Britain, France, and, to a lesser extent, Israel are robust societies, politically and economically. With the exception of Israel, the terrorist threat to these states is less existential than environmental.

The United Kingdom Experience[59]

Terrorism has historically been more of an internal problem for Britain than an international one. But internal in this context exceeds simply *domestic*, since much of Britain's experience of terrorism and counterterrorism has involved the struggle against nationalist revolutionaries in the heyday of the British Empire as well as in the intense period of decolonization after 1945. Only with the revival of political violence in Northern Ireland after 1969 has Britain faced a serious domestic terrorist challenge. Another and related aspect of the British experience has been the primacy of internal over military instruments in the fight against terrorism. Elements such as the Special Air Service (SAS) have taken part in counterterrorism operations, but the lead organizations have been and remain internal— Scotland Yard (especially the Special Branch and Specialist Operations Division), the Royal Ulster Constabulary, and above all the Security Service (MI-5).

Contemporary British thinking on counterterrorism tends to reflect the internal dimension that is most relevant to the United Kingdom (UK). Not surprisingly, British military thinking also focuses on internal risks, especially in the context of Northern Ireland and the spillover of Provisional IRA violence in Britain and against UK forces in Germany. A secondary, residual influence on British military doctrine flows from the colonial and postcolonial counterinsurgency experience. In general, there is a strong preference at all levels to give the police forces the central role in countering terrorism (this was true even in relation to counterinsurgency campaigns). With respect to counterterrorism, the military is always seen—in the British military vernacular—to be "acting in support of the civil authority." It is noteworthy that Royal Air Force (RAF) basic doctrine makes no men-

---

[59]I am grateful to Bruce Hoffman for his contribution to this discussion, much of which reflects his research and analysis.

tion whatsoever of counterterrorism as a role for air power.[60] British Army doctrine does refer to it, but almost exclusively in the context of counterinsurgency operations (i.e., countering terrorism as a tactic employed by insurgents).[61]   This is in marked contrast to the doctrinal approach within the U.S. military, which tends to identify terrorism as a separate and specific type of low-intensity conflict.

Where Britain has employed military power for counterterrorist, or more broadly counterinsurgency, purposes, the consistent keynote has been the use of "minimum force" and close integration of intelligence and operations with civil authorities. This approach has been assessed by some observers as making a virtue of necessity, given the increasingly serious constraints on British defense manpower and resources in the postwar period. The close integration and use of local resources has been another key feature of the British approach in various counterterrorism settings.

British forces, including the RAF, have had to address serious force protection risks arising from the Provisional IRA's campaign of attacks on military facilities in the UK and Germany. The Ministry of Defense and the services have invested heavily in countering IRA bombing tactics. The principal lesson of this experience has been that it is very difficult, even for sophisticated and highly motivated security establishments, to keep ahead of incremental evolutions in terrorist tactics and technology.[62]

In the European context, Britain has been relatively well-disposed toward multilateral action against international terrorism, and on numerous occasions has severed relations with state sponsors, including Libya, Syria, and Iran. London has also been broadly supportive of U.S.-led diplomatic, economic, and military initiatives in the counterterrorism arena, most notably in providing logistic support for the 1986 Operation El Dorado Canyon.[63] The UK has not,

---

[60]Royal Air Force, *AP300—Air Operations*, London (undated).

[61]See DGD&D, 18/34/56, Army Code 71596, *Army Field Manual*, Vol. V, *Operations Other than War (Counter Insurgency Operations)*, p. 3–4.

[62]For a detailed discussion of IRA measures and British countermeasures, see Chapter Two.

[63]See David Bonner, "The United Kingdom Response to Terrorism" in Paul Wilkinson (ed.), *Terrorism: British Perspectives*, Aldershot, Dartmouth, UK, 1993.

with a few specialized exceptions, deployed its military forces in direct counterterrorist missions. Elite units such as the SAS have reportedly advised local forces on hostage rescue operations, notably in Mogadishu (1977) and in Lima (1996–1997).

To date, neither IRA terrorism nor spillovers of Middle Eastern terrorism on British territory have posed an existential threat to British security. Britain's counterterrorism efforts may be judged as successful if the containment of casualties and economic disruption are taken as measures of success. The latter objective has come under pressure in recent years as IRA attacks on the mainland have come to focus on economic targets, including the disruption of rail, road, and air transport, bomb attacks in the City of London, and plans to sabotage electric power facilities.[64] The attractiveness of London as a target for economic terrorism, even for far-flung groups with agendas unrelated to British policy, may be a defining feature of future terrorist risks facing Britain.

The French Experience

Like Britain, France has long dealt with terrorism in both its internal and international dimensions as a consequence of colonialism and a stressful process of decolonization. France has had to address terrorist risks emanating from the Algerian revolution (both Algerian nationalists and French "ultras"), as well as more generalized spillovers of political violence from Middle Eastern conflicts. In the 1970s, France, in common with other West European states, faced a low-key threat from leftist terrorist groups such as Action Direct. More recently, France has felt the spillover effects of a new wave of Islamist violence, reaction, and anarchy in Algeria. Less prominent, but of considerable importance in relation to force protection for the French military, has been the ongoing campaign of terrorism by Corsican separatists.

French counterterrorism strategy has been guided by two basic principles. First, domestic terrorism is treated as subversion, with a

---

[64]Warren Hoge, "Britain Convicts Six in Plot to Black Out London," *New York Times*, July 3, 1997.

heavy emphasis on judicial investigation.[65]   Arguably, the leading actors in French counterterrorism efforts are not politicians or generals but magistrates.[66]   Intelligence for counterterrorism has received high priority and much attention is paid to the social roots of extremism and political violence, attention encouraged by the large pool of disaffected North Africans in French suburbs and their potential radicalization. In general, these fears have not materialized, although young North Africans have been implicated in terrorist attacks linked to the Algerian crisis.[67] The focus on roots of terrorism has helped shape French attitudes toward international initiatives, including the U.S.-organized March 1996 terrorism summit in Sharm al-Shayk, which French officials felt paid too little attention to underlying stresses in the region.[68]

Second, and more significantly, France has pursued a "sanctuary doctrine" aimed at isolating the country from international terrorism through neutrality and promotion of the idea that terrorists have "nothing to achieve and nothing to fear" in France.[69] This doctrine, applied with considerable vigor and with some success through the 1970s, has been difficult to sustain since the 1980s. On the one hand, the movement toward deeper European cooperation in the fight against terrorism has compelled France to adopt a multilateral approach, through the Trevi Group and other fora, in which France's exposure to terrorism is more difficult to control. On the other hand, the doctrine of sanctuary cannot function when France is the target of choice. The latest experience of Algerian-related terrorism is a clear example. Activists connected with Algeria's GIA (Armed Islamic Group) have engaged in a bombing campaign in the Paris Metro and

---

[65]Michel Wieviorka, "French Politics and Strategy on Terrorism," in Barry Rubin (ed.), *The Politics of Counter-Terrorism: The Ordeal of Democratic States*, School of Advanced International Studies, Washington, DC, 1990, p. 68.

[66]See Jean-Louis Bruguiere, "La Menace Terroriste," *Defense Nationale*, April 1996; and Craig R. Whitney, "France's 'Cowboy' Judge: A Relentless Tracker of International Terrorists," *International Herald Tribune*, December 5, 1996.

[67]With the large numbers of disaffected Algerians in French cities, some experts have expressed surprise that France has not seen many more extremist attacks.

[68]Jose Garcon and Jean-Pierre Perrin, "Terrorism: Serious French-U.S. Disagreement," *Liberation*, FBIS, March 27, 1996; and "Sharm al-Shayk Summit Reaction," FBIS, March 15, 1996.

[69]Wieviorka, 1990, p. 68.

elsewhere not out of convenience, but out of well-calculated symbolism and a desire to affect French perceptions.

French observers stress the manpower-intensive nature of counterterrorist operations, in terms of both surveillance and presence, and tend to be skeptical of technology as a solution. French policy, especially in the wake of terrorist bombings in Paris, places considerable emphasis on public reassurance, which has led to a large-scale presence of police, gendarmerie, and regular military forces on French streets. This last dimension has touched off an active debate within the country on the implications for civil-military relations. The memory of a near coup organized by right-wing officers angered at the perceived abandonment of Algeria under de Gaulle still haunts the intellectual debate on this issue in France.

In some respects, France comes closest to the United States in its exposure and concern about force protection. France has a long experience in countering terrorist threats to its military forces abroad, from its colonial days to losses in Lebanon and elsewhere. French NGOs such as Medecins Sans Frontieres have also confronted this problem directly in Somalia and other crisis zones, and this experience has been examined with interest by military planners. French force protection efforts have developed alongside a doctrine of expeditionary warfare, with similarities to the way in which American strategy is evolving. Within France, the principal force protection challenge arises from the activity of Corsican separatists.[70] This has been a special concern for the French Air Force at Solenzara air base (built by the United States in 1944). Both the base and the local electric power infrastructure have been targeted by terrorists. The Algerian bombings in Paris, while not aimed at the military, have also compelled the armed forces to take the force protection mission seriously.

French analysts see Algerian extremists, in Algeria, in France, and elsewhere in Europe, as exemplars of the "new" terrorism. The ex-

---

[70]Some dozen factions of Corsican extremists have been responsible for roughly 100 deaths over the past two decades. Most of the incidents have been on the island of Corsica, although several recent incidents on the mainland are regarded by French officials as a disturbing development. "Government Determined to Combat Corsican Terrorism," FBIS, October 8, 1996; and Craig R. Whitney, "Corsicans Say They Set Weekend Bomb on French Mainland," *New York Times*, October 8, 1996.

tremists are characterized by loose networks rather than hierarchical structures, with many acts seemingly the work of freelance individuals or small units—although often tied to the resources and expertise of more professional activists, with many cut-outs. Although the bulk of Algerian-inspired terrorism on both sides of the Mediterranean has been carried out through conventional, even primitive means, at least one incident involved radiological material in Paris.

To the extent that France has historically been able to manage, if not really to insulate itself from, terrorist risks to its territory and its forces abroad, its counterterrorism policy has been largely successful. Terrorism has not posed an existential threat to French society since the Algerian conflict in the 1950s and early 1960s. Nonetheless, France faces difficult adjustments to its policy, arising from a continuing decline in the viability of the "sanctuary" doctrine and growing exposure to spillovers of political violence emanating from across the Mediterranean and, potentially, from France's own immigrant population. French strategists are also increasingly concerned about the potential for "superterrorism" involving WMD. Here too, France's proximity to North Africa and its history of political involvement in the region raises the specter of terrorism being used as a WMD delivery system against the background of confrontation with a rogue regime.

With regard to force protection, France's willingness to employ limited force for political management on a global basis suggests an exposure not unlike that of the United States. Indeed, the presence of French and U.S. forces in regions of shared interest (e.g., the Balkans and the Gulf), with increasingly similar expeditionary strategies, suggests considerable potential for future cooperation.

The Israeli Experience

For Israel, terrorism is an extension of war, and counterterrorism is often and naturally discussed as part of a "war paradigm." Israel's exposure to terrorism is long-standing and intensive, and perhaps as a result various myths have arisen with regard to Israeli counterterrorism policy. These myths include the notion of "no negotiation" and the doctrine of preemption and prompt retaliation. Both doctrines have frayed to the point of being unrecognizable. Israel has, in fact, negotiated in detail with a variety of Palestinian and Shi'ite groups over prisoner exchanges and other matters. More broadly, Israel is engaged in a more or less continuous process of signaling and bargaining in the cycle of terrorism and response. Not all terrorist attacks on Israel provoke a response, and much of Israel's counterterrorism activity is aimed at preemption, prevention, and disruption rather than simple retaliation. It has been suggested that the essential difference between Israeli and American approaches to counterterrorism is that the former is definably "offensive" while the latter has had the luxury of being "defensive" or reactive in character.[71] Developments over the past decade suggest that this distinction has lost much of its validity (if indeed it was ever valid), as Israeli policy becomes more complex and U.S. policy becomes more aggressive.

Israeli observers stress that because of the compact size of the society and the classification of terrorism as a first-order threat to the security of the state, the Israeli public, even more than Americans or Europeans, see any successful terrorist incident by definition as a failure of counterterrorism policy. At the same time, the ongoing nature of terrorism compels Israeli policymakers to spend enormous energy on reassurance and the management of terrorism as a public relations problem as well as a physical threat.

According to senior Israeli officials, current counterterrorism priorities are (in this order): intelligence, operational capabilities for counterterrorism, and protection. There is a strong intelligence emphasis on humint over technical means. Operational capabilities include, above all, the capacity for preventive action, both covert and military. Protection implies measures for close-in defense and the mitigation of damage and casualties. Like their French counterparts, Israeli officials and analysts stress the manpower-intensive nature of the counterterrorism mission, although Israel has devoted considerable energy to the application of sensor technology to surveillance and interdiction.[72]

---

[71]This distinction is made in Charles Wise and Stephen Sloan, "Countering Terrorism: The U.S. and Israeli Approach," *Middle East Review*, Spring 1977.

[72]Including the visible use of sensors (and dummy sensors) for deterrence and canalization.

Israeli officials and analysts are among the most sensitive to the potential for unconventional terrorism (the term is understood in Israel to include suicide bombings), including the use of WMD. Factors such as Israeli geography, the intermixture of Arab and Israeli populations, and the capacity of regional terrorist networks and their supporters lead Israeli experts to worry, foremost, about chemical agents, and only secondarily about biological and nuclear terrorism.[73] It is widely assumed that regional adversaries bent on developing a nuclear capability will wish to hold this card as a component of national power, rather than covertly transfer it to a terrorist organization. That said, it might be possible for adversaries to use terrorists as a primitive delivery system for nuclear weapons, in which case there would be the potential for WMD terrorism to trigger a state-to-state exchange.

The notion of a "new" terrorism, characterized by diffuse networks and unclear sponsorship, is actively debated in Israel. However, Israeli strategy, like that of other Western states—but perhaps particularly the United States—faces a difficult adjustment in this context. Like the United States, Israel has traditionally viewed the application of sanctions and, ultimately, the use of force against state sponsors and terrorist leaderships as a central component of counterterrorism strategy.[74] This made sense in relation to the bureaucratic and hierarchical terrorist organizations Israel has confronted in previous decades. The Israeli air attack on the PLO headquarters at Hamman-Lif near Tunis in October 1985 was aimed at disrupting the routine workings of an organization with payrolls, file cabinets, and conference rooms—as well as sending a strong signal of resolve. Few if any of the terrorist networks Israel confronts today present such targets. The Tunis raid, and the 1982 intervention in Lebanon, were exemplars of an increasingly anachronistic strategy aimed at forms of terrorist organization and behavior that have largely disappeared. With the exception of the situation in southern Lebanon (which has less to do with terrorism and more to do with an insur-

---

[73]For a discussion of the general problem, see Gerald M. Steinberg, "Israeli Responses to the Threat of Chemical Warfare," *Armed Forces and Society*, Fall 1993.

[74]See Boaz Ganor, *Countering State-Sponsored Terrorism*, International Policy Institute for Counter-Terrorism, Herzaliya, Israel, 1997.

gency), Israel's counterterrorism strategy is increasingly a struggle against individuals and networks.

Despite the images derived from the Tunis attack, Israeli air power has rarely been employed in a true counterterrorism mode.[75] The Israeli military speaks of operations in southern Lebanon as "counterterrorism," but again, the environment is shaped by an insurgency against well-armed and organized irregular forces, with political constraints on the use of force. As in many other cases of low-intensity conflict, terrorist tactics make an appearance alongside other conventional and unconventional modes of war.[76] It also appears that Hizbullah has responded to Israel's air superiority, and military superiority in general, with a horizontal terror strategy, retaliating for Israeli air strikes through terrorist attacks against Israeli and Jewish targets elsewhere, often far afield. The devastating 1994 bombing of the Jewish center in Buenos Aires, for example, is seen by some analysts as a horizontal response to a previous series of Israeli strikes against Hizbullah targets. Some also view it as successful in deterring more extensive Israeli strikes against the Hizbullah leadership.

Has Israeli counterterrorism policy been successful in strategic terms? Not surprisingly, Israeli observers are divided on this question. Terrorism has not eliminated the state of Israel, so the most extreme terrorist objective has clearly been thwarted. But most terrorism aimed at Israel has had more limited goals. It is true that Israel has outlasted most of the terrorist groups with which it has been engaged over the last decades, but terrorist groups have their

---

[75]Israel has reportedly used airborne electronic countermeasures to interfere with Hizbullah radio-controlled bombs, with declining success as Hizbullah developed sophisticated "just in time" arming. These bombings reportedly achieved effectiveness rates as high as 50 percent against Israeli military traffic. Douglas Jehl, "With Iran's Aid, Guerrillas Gain Against Israelis," *New York Times*, February 26, 1997. See also David Eshel, "Counterguerrilla Warfare in South Lebanon," *Marine Corps Gazette*, July 1997.

[76]It is noteworthy that even in this setting, Israel has found it difficult to capitalize on its dominance of the air. The introduction of Stinger-type munitions has complicated the picture. Israel has made extensive use of unmanned aerial vehicles (UAVs) in conjunction with air and artillery operations in southern Lebanon, with mixed success. There is a perception that UAVs have performed well but cannot offset many of the fundamental constraints on air power in the south Lebanon environment, where guerrilla attacks are often launched from populated areas.

own life cycles and the systemic threat remains. Realistic strategists have characterized the true Israeli objective as living with terrorism, not eliminating it.[77] By this measure, Israeli success is mixed. Existential threats to the state have been avoided, but the future of the society and the overall quality of Israeli security are still driven to a great extent by the effects of terrorism in Israel and its surrounding region.[78] Even by the narrow measure of "maintaining political freedom of action," the judgment is increasingly gloomy. The death of Prime Minister Rabin through terrorism and the ongoing campaign of suicide bombings has had profound consequences for the peace process and has set the limits on political change. Arguably, Israeli counterterrorism policy is now driven more by tactical considerations of personal security than by strategic objectives.

Allied Perspectives on Terrorist Challenges Facing the United States

The U.S. position vis-à-vis terrorism and force protection risks is followed closely and widely discussed in Britain, France, and Israel. Several perspectives stand out. First, experts and officials in all three countries believe that the terrorist threat to U.S. forces and other targets in the Gulf region is bound to deepen. For the most part, the United States is seen as a secondary but symbolic target of regime opponents. In some cases, as with bin Laden, the expulsion of Western forces from the Gulf region, and especially Saudi Arabia, has emerged as an objective in its own right. For Iraq and Iran, any large-scale presence of U.S. forces will present a lucrative target for terrorism, aimed at keeping Washington off balance and perhaps satisfying less-rational needs for revenge. Under these conditions, a reduction in presence and movement toward an expeditionary model for rapid deployment in crises is seen as appropriate. For both British and

---

[77]This point was made forcefully in Hanan Alon, *Countering Palestinian Terrorism in Israel: Toward a Policy Analysis of Countermeasures*, RAND, N-1567-FF, 1980. The study concludes that terrorism cannot be eradicated by countermeasures, and therefore policy should be directed toward limiting casualties.

[78]Terrorism can have disproportionately destabilizing effects in fundamentally unstable regions such as the Middle East. See Yehezkel Dror, "Terrorism in Meta-Stable Environments: The Middle East," paper prepared for Begin-Sadaf Center for Strategic Studies, Bar-Ilan University, Conference on Middle East Terrorism, Israel, May 26, 1997.

French observers, the U.S. experience in the Gulf suggests parallels with their own past as security managers in the Middle East (e.g., the Mahdist attacks on British forces in Sudan at the turn of the century). Notably, Israeli officials and observers do not speak in terms of "force protection" as a distinctive problem or mission. Israel's small size and pervasive military reserve system encourage a seamless view of the Israeli Defense Forces and civilian society as potential terrorist targets. Again, south Lebanon is perhaps an exception, but here the problem is in the nature of an insurgency. The terrorist risk facing U.S. forces deployed overseas has no real parallel in Israeli experience.

Second, there is a widespread perception that U.S. technology and organizational innovation are driving the "revolution in military affairs," with an ever-increasing gap between the U.S. military and all other defense establishments in the capacity for conventional war fighting. British, French, and Israeli militaries also exhibit characteristics of this revolution, but the United States is likely to remain the exemplar. As the United States (and the West generally) become more capable than their regional adversaries, terrorism and other forms of unconventional warfare as an asymmetric strategy will become more attractive. Because of the logistical and coalition dimensions of U.S. power projection activities, there is some concern that terrorism in the "war paradigm" aimed at the United States will inevitably affect U.S. allies in Europe and the Middle East. Closer cooperation on counterterrorism strategies may be a key feature of coalition strategy in this environment and may indeed be necessary to prevent terrorist risks from complicating arrangements for access and overflight in crises. Few European or Israeli analysts view Saddam Hussein's failure to mobilize a terrorist front in the Gulf War with complacency, and the continued prospect of Iraqi involvement in terrorist activities is cited as a key question for the future.

A third theme in British, French, and Israeli perception is a degree of skepticism about the ability of technology to counter terrorist threats. Without dismissing the utility of technical means for intelligence gathering, surveillance, and preventive action, analysts in all three countries emphasize the inherently manpower-intensive nature of the antiterrorist mission, especially in civilian settings. Even in force protection, where technology can contribute substantially to the defense of fixed installations, Israeli interlocutors especially insist that "beyond the perimeter" approaches are critical. One high-ranking Israeli policymaker expressed the view that the best force protection investment for the United States in the Gulf (or elsewhere) would be the assiduous cultivation of influential elites at the local level, building a constituency with a stake in a continued and secure U.S. presence.

Lessons of the Allied Experience

Despite many differences of exposure and perspective, we can identify a few key lessons of the allied experience that are relevant to U.S. and USAF strategy and planning:

- Terrorist risks cannot be eliminated, only contained and managed.

- Effective counterterrorism strategies must address the problem of networks and individuals, not just state sponsors.

- Terrorists tend to innovate in an evolutionary rather than a revolutionary manner in their attacks on military forces and other targets, staying just ahead of countermeasures.

- There is an imperative of close coordination among intelligence, civilian, and military agencies.

- More expeditionary approaches to force protection are needed to accompany expeditionary approaches to power projection.

CONCEPTUALIZING NATIONAL COUNTERTERRORISM STRATEGY

Discussions about counterterrorism and its strategies are generally conducted in isolation. Perhaps because terrorism is often treated in emotive terms and tends to strike directly at society's sense of security, the struggle against terrorism is frequently seen as an objective in its own right, divorced from broader national security concerns. A more comprehensive approach would place terrorist risks in the context of other risks to national security and would place counterterrorism in the context of other international security—or even "grand strategic"—aims. In short, we should approach U.S. counterterrorism strategy with an eye on the broader security environment, as well as the full range of instruments—diplomatic, economic, military, and covert—at the disposal of policymakers. Above all, counterterrorism strategy must address the challenges posed by the "new" terrorism—more lethal; increasingly networked; more diverse in terms of motivations, sponsorship, and security consequences; and more global in reach.

One suitable framework, developed at RAND for conceptualizing national counterterrorism strategy, treats the problem in three dimensions: "core" strategy, or furthering the most critical objectives over the longer term; "environment shaping," or fostering the conditions for day-to-day counterterrorism success; and "hedging," or reducing exposure and mitigating the consequences in anticipation of counterterrorism failures.[79] In some areas, air and space power can make a significant contribution to a national counterterrorism strategy. In other areas, its contribution will be limited. As the nature of terrorism has changed, the utility of air and space power is also changing in ways that may render some of the stock images of deterrence and compulsion increasingly anachronistic.

Core Strategy

National counterterrorism strategy should include four core elements: reducing the systemic causes, deterring terrorists and their sponsors, reducing the risk of "superterrorism," and retaliating where deterrence fails. These elements address the longer-term terrorist risk to broader U.S. security interests (e.g., regional stability and freedom of action) as well as special, sharper threats to national security (e.g., terrorist use of WMD).

• *First, political violence, including terrorism, has systemic origins that can be ameliorated.* Social and economic pressures, frustrated political aspirations, and in a more proximate sense, the personal experiences of terrorists and their relations, all contribute to the terrorist reservoir. As one strategist has noted, "terrorism is not ubiquitous and neither is it uncontainable, but the potential for its

---

[79]This tripartite framework for strategic planning is developed in several RAND analyses by Paul Davis, Paul Bracken, Zalmay Khalilzad, and others. See Paul K. Davis, *National Security in an Era of Uncertainty*, RAND, P-7605, 1989.

occurrence is virtually as widespread as is the manifestation of bitter political antagonisms . . . reduce the latter and you will reduce, though not eliminate, the former."[80] That said, policies aimed at reducing the systemic causes for terrorism are by their very nature longer-term instruments. The failure of regimes to provide for peaceful political change and the phenomenon of economies unable to keep pace with population growth and demands for more evenly distributed benefits can provide fertile ground for extremism and political violence affecting U.S. interests. For this reason, the United States has a stake in promoting political and economic reform as a means of reducing the potential for terrorism, some of which, as in Latin America, the Middle East, and the Gulf, may be directed at us.

Similarly, unresolved ethnic and nationalist conflicts have traditionally been a leading source of terrorism. Diplomacy and the use of force can contribute both to the containment and the eventual resolution of such conflicts, whether in the context of the Palestinian issue, nationalist confrontations in the Balkans or the Caucasus, or ethnic frictions in Africa. Left unresolved, these confrontations will persist as flashpoints for local and international terrorism. Incorporating policies aimed at reducing the body of grievances behind terrorism does not imply any reduction in the taboo against terrorism as a tactic or sympathy for terrorists. It simply treats terrorism as we would other sources of conflict and threats to security, by giving first priority to prevention.

It is unlikely that air and space power can contribute significantly to national strategy in this area, which is largely the province of diplomacy and economic policy, and has more to do with the reform of societies than threat or use of force. Indirectly, however, air power can bolster the security of societies against external threats (as with our Gulf allies or Israel) and permit greater attention to domestic problems—if governments choose to do so intelligently. Where strategies for forestalling domestic and regional conflict fail, as in "pre-Dayton" Bosnia, air power can support peacekeeping, peacemaking, and humanitarian assistance and perhaps reduce the longer-term scope for terrorism and political violence.

---

[80]Colin S. Gray, "Combating Terrorism," *Parameters*, Autumn 1993, p. 20.

• *A second core objective of counterterrorism strategy should be to strengthen and deepen deterrence.* This is a less and less straightforward challenge as terrorists and their sponsors become more diverse and diffuse. Against state sponsors, where these still exist in the traditional sense and can be identified, the most effective approach may be to find targets of value to the regime in the most direct sense, the loss of which would threaten the leadership's hold on power. More generalized diplomatic, economic, or military initiatives aimed at isolation or inflicting pain and embarrassment face many obstacles when the sponsor is a totalitarian or rogue regime. With the most extreme rogues, such as Libya or Iraq, there is the deeper question of whether their behavior, including the sponsorship of terrorism, can be deterred at all—a dilemma that takes on greater significance if we consider terrorism with weapons of mass destruction. Many analyses have addressed the difficulty of applying rational and ethnocentric strategic concepts to "crazy" states.[81] In this setting, deterrence probably cannot be subtle. To be effective, the threat posed may need to be massive and "personal" to the leadership. Qaddafi's Libya is perhaps the best example of this. As noted earlier, the El Dorado Canyon raid may not have deterred Qaddafi from further involvement in international terrorism, but it probably did deter him from the open activity characteristic before 1986.

In contrast, Syrian and Iranian support for terrorism does not follow the "crazy" state model. In both cases, and most clearly for Syria, sponsorship of terrorism continues to serve national and regime interests. Damascus views its ties to terrorist groups as a means of leverage in relations with Israel, Turkey, other Arab states, and the West. It is a card to be kept, used, or traded away as circumstances dictate. As with Iraq, the propensity to become involved with terrorist movements may also flow from the oppressive security culture within the country or the natural link between "state terrorism" and the use of terrorism as an instrument beyond the state's borders. For Iran, international terrorism involvement might best be seen as a product of a "violent and unstable political history" (true of many states in the region) and the dictates of internal politics in the wake

---

[81]See most notably, Yehezkel Dror, *Crazy States: A Counterconventional Strategic Problem*, Kraus, Milwood, New York, 1980. See also Steven Metz, "Deterring Conflict Short of War," *Strategic Review*, Fall 1994.

of the revolution—"an instrument of neither first nor last resort."[82] Support for terrorism in this case has rational, if unacceptable, underpinnings, so a more diverse range of tactics can be useful to deter it, including embarrassment, isolation, and denial of key political and economic goals. Indeed, it is arguable that Iraqi, Iranian, and Syrian support for terrorism is a product of perceived strategic weakness and relative weakness in conventional military terms vis-à-vis the United States, Israel, and the West—a sort of ongoing asymmetric strategy. To the extent that Iraq, Iran, and Syria develop stronger conventional and unconventional military capabilities, they may actually find the terrorist instrument less attractive—and turn to different, perhaps more serious challenges for the United States.

In some cases, as in Afghanistan and Sudan, state behavior may constitute a gray area, with tolerance for terrorist activity short of outright sponsorship. Such a regime may not be a U.S. target for preemption or retaliation, but it cannot expect to enjoy immunity from counterterrorist attacks or other sanctions.

Air power has been and will likely continue to be a preferred instrument for striking state sponsors where U.S. interests are directly threatened. This capacity for preemption and retaliation, as demonstrated in Libya and Iraq, supports deterrence vis-à-vis state sponsors, especially where the calculus is more rational than "crazy."

Looking beyond state sponsors, the task of deterrence becomes more difficult but also more imperative given trends in the nature of terrorism. Most observers agree that traditional state sponsorship, while still a factor in key instances, is waning. The "new" terrorism is characterized by more diffuse groups with hazier links to sponsors, many of whom may be nonstate actors in their own right. As a result, the central problem for deterrence is likely to be dealing with individuals and networks rather than states and hierarchical terrorist organizations—as illustrated dramatically by the events of August 1998. A shorthand for this challenge might be "personalized" deterrence. Our counterterrorism policy already shows an inclination in this direction, air power will very likely support this

---

[82]Jerrold D. Green, "Terrorism and Politics in Iran," in Martha Crenshaw (ed.), *Terrorism in Context*, Pennsylvania State University Press, University Park, Pennsylvania, 1995, pp. 593–594.

dimension in the future, with consequent requirements for technological leverage in dealing with small actors, even individuals, often in urban settings. Tasks in this setting would include the extraterritorial apprehension of terrorist suspects (as in the forcing down of Achille Lauro hijacking suspects over the Mediterranean at Sigonella), or the return of terrorists caught in far-flung places, with or without the cooperation of host countries.[83] The recent capture in Pakistan of the alleged perpetrator in the lethal shooting outside CIA headquarters provides another example along these lines. More generally, things of value to terrorists and their sponsors as individuals can be identified and held at risk, through the use of force or, equally, through administrative or information means. The targets might be bank accounts, safe-houses, or the individuals themselves. Personalizing our counterterrorism strategy suggests many possible tactics other than outright assassination, which is an unattractive and legally constrained policy and is, on balance, incompatible with U.S. interests.[84]

In seeking to end state sponsorship and to tailor deterrence to the growing role of individuals and networks in international terrorism, we should also be aware of potential and unintended consequences of success. State-sponsored terrorism has historically been among the most conservative in its tactics, and state sponsors may sometimes constrain the behavior of violent groups. If extremist groups shift from state sponsorship to the patronage of wealthy sympathizers or nonstate actors with criminal connections, the net result may be less restraint and greater lethality. That said, this trend is already well under way and has little to do with increased pressure on

---

[83]Presidential Directive PD-39, in its publicly released version, notes that "if we do not receive adequate cooperation from a state that harbors a terrorist whose extradition we are seeking, we shall take appropriate measures to induce cooperation" . . . "Return of suspects by force may be effected without the cooperation of the host country." See Bryan Bender, "U.S. May Use Force to Nab Terrorists Overseas," *Defense Daily*, January 31, 1997, and "Policy on Terror Suspects Overseas," *Washington Post*, February 5, 1997. The treatment of such activities under international law is addressed in Jimmy Gurule, "Terrorism, Territorial Sovereignty, and the Forcible Apprehension of International Criminals Abroad," *Hastings International and Comparative Law Review*, Vol. 17, p. 457.

[84]For a full discussion of the pros and cons of assassination, see Brian Michael Jenkins, *Should Our Arsenal Against Terrorism Include Assassination?* RAND, P-7303, 1987.

state sponsors. Similarly, in targeting network nodes and key individuals—personalizing deterrence—we may confront some undesirable consequences of such "decapitation." The experience of left-wing terrorism in Europe in the 1970s suggests that splintered and compartmentalized groups may be more violent, in part to demonstrate that they have not lost their ability to act.[85] Certainly, the current fragmented terrorism in Algeria exceeds in its violence anything committed by more coherent terrorist organizations in recent years. Yet it can be argued that the new, networked model of terrorist organization has arisen for reasons of its own and is by definition less affected by the loss of individuals. Such organizations cannot be decapitated in the traditional sense, but their effectiveness can be reduced by interfering with key nodes (people) in the infrastructure and removing key operatives from circulation.

• *A third, and increasingly important "core" objective will be to reduce the risk of "superterrorism" involving weapons of mass destruction.* This is, above all, a problem of homeland defense for the United States, and perhaps the most serious homeland defense challenge in the post–Cold War environment. Indeed, the United States as a global power has a stake in containing this risk worldwide, not just on U.S. territory, since a devastating terrorist use of WMD— especially a nuclear device—would transform security perceptions and strategic reality everywhere. The potential for WMD terrorism has emerged as a driving force behind the public debate on terrorism and counterterrorism policy, as well as recent U.S. government initiatives on the same issues.[86] Nuclear, biological, chemical, or radiological attacks by terrorists, acting alone or as part of a sponsored strike against the United States, could cause mass casualties as well as immense economic and social disruption in urban areas. Military facilities, including air bases, will be vulnerable, although WMD attacks are unlikely to prove effective unless they are near or on the

---

[85]See Martha Crenshaw, "The Unintended Consequences of Counter-terrorism Policies," unpublished paper prepared for the Council on Foreign Relations Roundtable on Terrorism, New York, 1997.

[86]The Defense Science Board and the National Defense Panel have focused on WMD and transnational risks in recent studies. A good general discussion of the need for national attention to this problem can be found in *Terrorism, Weapons of Mass Destruction, and U.S. Security*, 1997 Sam Nunn Policy Forum (Executive Summary), University of Georgia, Athens, Georgia, 1997.

base. The global control and surveillance of WMD-related materials (and expertise) is an important objective. If state adversaries are manufacturing agents of mass destruction that could be delivered by terrorist means, preemptive action could be required, with consequent demands on air power for the attack of hardened targets. Specialized intelligence activities, in cooperation with allied states, are essential for warning, control, and intervention in this inherently global problem area.

• *Fourth, the United States must have the capacity and willingness to retaliate against terrorists and their sponsors when deterrence and preventive measures fail.* With the increasing lethality of international terrorism, the question of retaliation can be expected to loom even larger in the perceptions of policymakers and the public. A demonstrated willingness to retaliate makes an obvious contribution to deterrence, especially in relation to state sponsors with much to lose, but also serves less-tangible purposes. Retaliation, including the use of air power as in Operation El Dorado Canyon, as in Afghanistan and Sudan, can serve an important cathartic purpose, and reassures the public and international opinion that terrorism against U.S. interests does not fall below the threshold of U.S. action. As in the consideration of deterrence, the principal challenge for the future is likely to be the adaptation of our retaliatory policies and techniques to deal with individuals, nonstate actors, and terrorist networks. Again, in many cases the appropriate response may not be the physical destruction of targets, but rather strikes against information and resources.

It is worth noting here that terrorism itself can be a constraint on the use of force, including air power, by the United States in regional contingencies. Terrorist action against facilities, personnel, and equipment, either deployed or en route, is one problem. Another problem is posed by the demonstrated tendency of adversaries under threat of U.S. air strikes to take hostages as a means of deterring attacks. Saddam Hussein resorted to this tactic during Desert Shield, and Bosnian Serb commanders held UN peacekeepers for similar purposes. The likelihood that adversaries, especially weak adversaries, will employ such tactics in the future reinforces the need for accurate intelligence and surveillance, highly discrete targeting, and nonlethal technologies.

Environment Shaping

The core dimensions of counterterrorism strategy will need to be supported by a range of policies aimed at containing near-term risks and fostering the conditions for ongoing success. Several of these policies have implications for air and space power.

• *Make international terrorism more transparent.* Air and space power can contribute to the embarrassment and isolation of traditional state sponsors by making their support for terrorism more transparent to U.S. policymakers and world opinion. Examples are the use of space-based surveillance, reconnaissance aircraft, and unmanned aerial vehicles to expose terrorist camps or other forms of state or nonstate assistance. Overhead imagery helped explain the U.S. action against terrorist targets in Afghanistan. This is likely to be a key, high-leverage role for air and space power, and can have a synergistic effect with other counterterrorism instruments. Similarly, the actions of terrorist organizations and networks of individuals can be monitored from space and the information used by the United States or shared, where appropriate, to forestall terrorist attacks or to identify critical nodes in the terrorist infrastructure. While it may be argued that this is largely the province of humint, the growing reliance of terrorist networks on modern information flows introduces new possibilities for surveillance and intelligence gathering by technical means short of space-based reconnaissance. The ability to make terrorism more transparent can help to build the case for coordinated, international responses to terrorist networks or to state sponsors, where otherwise evidence is often murky and insufficient to mobilize allied policymakers (as has been the case vis-à-vis Iran).[87] Air and space power can also serve force protection in increasingly risk-prone environments such as the Gulf and Central America.

• *Shrink zones of chaos and terrorist sanctuary.*[88] Just as reducing the root causes of terrorism is a core objective, so should we change the conditions in areas that have offered terrorists safe havens and bases for transnational operations. Afghanistan, Sudan, Northern Iraq, and

---

[87]The utility of exposing covert aggression to public view as a preparation for U.S. action against state sponsors is discussed in Stephen T. Hosmer and George K. Tanham, *Countering Covert Aggression*, RAND, N-2412-USDP, 1986, pp. 11–12.

[88]I am grateful to my RAND colleague Zalmay Khalilzad for this formulation.

Syrian-controlled areas of Lebanon are leading examples. In another setting, conditions in Colombia offer similar refuge. We must prevent the emergence of new zones of chaos and sanctuary. As noted earlier, there is significant potential for this in parts of the Balkans, the Caucasus, and Central Asia. Where domestic terrorism is rife, as in Algeria, there will also be a risk of cross-border activity. At the diplomatic level, we should be keenly aware of the risks inherent in allowing political vacuums to exist, with no clear-cut exercise of sovereignty. Such areas will be the natural operating environment for violent nonstate actors and terrorist networks. To the extent that notions of spreading anarchy on the periphery of the developed world prove correct, the problem of terrorist-friendly zones may become more widespread. Governments presiding over sanctuaries, whether within their own territory (as in Sudan) or across their borders (as with Syria's role in Lebanon) must understand that closing down terrorist bases and expelling known activists are essential preconditions for any form of positive relations with the United States, and that continued tolerance of terrorist activity implies a high and continuing cost. With regard to the forcible apprehension of terrorist suspects, zones of chaos and sanctuary should be fair game for the United States and the international community. Large rewards for information on suspect individuals and groups in such areas may be effective.

• *Make counterterrorism an integral part of alliance strategies.* Alliance relationships in Europe and Asia are changing to reflect post–Cold War requirements. In parallel with the geographic enlargement of NATO, the Alliance is beginning to take up new missions, including peacekeeping and crisis management. Defense relationships with Japan, Israel, and even Russia are being driven in the direction of cooperation on security challenges rather than the defense of borders. Cooperation in the realm of counterterrorism should be high on the agenda for these evolving security relationships. In the case of NATO, this may require giving the Alliance a specific mandate to work in this area, since terrorism is still treated as a national responsibility. A coordinated approach to terrorism should be part of the broader dialogue on "third pillar" issues (crime, narcotics, migration, etc.) between Washington and the EU. If U.S. counterterrorism strategy concentrates on homeland defense against WMD terrorism and features more active efforts to apprehend suspects and preemptive action abroad, multilateral coordination will become essential if our policy is to avoid political frictions with allies.

• *Limit U.S. exposure worldwide, consistent with grand strategic objectives and operational requirements.* As a global power with pervasive economic and political interests, the United States will remain exposed to international terrorism. Although facilities can be hardened and tourists, businessmen, and diplomats can adjust their behavior to present less-attractive targets, the very scale and importance of the U.S. engagement overseas suggests this must be an "accepted vulnerability." With regard to the U.S. military presence, more explicit choices are possible. The movement toward an expeditionary model for presence and power projection has many sources, but must include the desire to limit terrorist risks as a constraint on U.S. freedom of action. In some instances, as in Korea, requirements for immediate forward defense make reliance on a purely expeditionary model for power projection difficult. In Europe, and perhaps elsewhere, political imperatives will drive the balance between permanent presence and power projection. In the Gulf, where terrorist risks are high and probably growing, the expeditionary model has considerable advantages. The resentments and frictions associated with a highly visible permanent presence may be reduced, limiting the incentives for terrorism directed at U.S. forces. At the same time, a more flexible and unpredictable approach to basing complicates the planning problem for terrorists bent on attacking U.S. facilities and personnel. The Air Expeditionary Force concept enjoys these and other advantages in relation to terrorist risks but also imposes new challenges for force protection, which must also become more expeditionary, adaptable, and conversant with conditions in advance of deployments to far-flung destinations.

USAF force protection efforts are part of the "hardening" task, and will contribute to U.S. counterterrorism strategy by reducing terrorism-related constraints on U.S. freedom of action. These efforts will be part of a larger global equation with regard to vulnerability and terrorists' choice of targets. Past terrorist behavior suggests a considerable degree of adaptability in tactics, with a natural preference for soft targets. If U.S. military forces deployed in the Gulf become harder, less-attractive targets, terrorists might shift their focus to U.S. diplomats and businessmen or the oil industry. This displacement effect of hardening on other targets in no sense reduces the rationale for better force protection—it simply suggests that counterterrorism must be viewed in a comprehensive manner, with full recognition of all consequences.

• *Target terrorist funding and networks.* As traditional patterns of state sponsorship wane and are overtaken by a much more diffuse type of sponsorship, with cut-outs and a greater role for nonstate sponsors, our counterterrorism policies must adapt accordingly. "Following the money" will help to identify sponsors and the terrorists themselves in this murkier environment. Understanding and severing the funding links between international crime and drug organizations and politically motivated terrorists will interrupt a major source of support for some of the most violent terrorist movements and make the most expensive and lethal technologies more difficult to acquire (e.g., agents of mass destruction, Stinger-class missiles). More diverse funding sources, including sympathetic individuals in the United States, also imply a larger group of potentially violent operatives.[89] To some extent, this linkage has already been borne out with the progression from fund-raising to international terrorist incidents on U.S. soil.

The propensity for terrorist groups to seek "private-sector" funding, often in parallel with apparently nonviolent social and political activities (Hamas provides an example), may encourage victims of terrorist acts to seek financial compensation from terrorist movements, their fund-raisers, and donors. The recent compensation paid by the PLO to the Klinghoffer family, relatives of the victim of the 1985 Achille Lauro hijacking, sets a useful precedent.[90] If donors to causes linked with terrorism become aware that their assets can be placed in jeopardy, their enthusiasm may well be dimmed.

Similarly, the propensity of modern terrorist movements to adopt network forms of organization in preference to more traditional, hierarchical patterns is to a great extent a consequence of the informa-

---

[89]Inadequate scrutiny and control of students from countries implicated in terrorism resident in the United States raises issues related to terrorist infrastructure as well as the leakage of technical expertise on weapons of mass destruction. Hillary Mann, *Open Admissions: U.S. Policy Toward Students from Terrorism-Supporting Countries in the Middle East,* Washington Institute for Near East Policy, Washington, DC, 1997.

[90]"PLO Settles with Family of Achille Lauro Victim," *Washington Post,* August 12, 1997.

tion revolution and the growing use of modern communications by terrorists. Indeed, concepts of "leaderless resistance" as espoused by anti-government militia groups in the United States or the highly compartmented cells seen in Hamas and other potent terrorist groups in the Middle East are greatly facilitated by encrypted phone communications and the Internet. This suggests that much of our counterterrorism effort in the future will be in the information warfare realm. Although networks will be more difficult to penetrate and disrupt than traditional groups, they too will have vulnerable nodes that can be targeted. Networks are likely to be required to fight networks, which argues for greater networking and coordination among counterterrorism services and agencies.[91]

Hedging Strategy

The third dimension of counterterrorism strategy accepts that however effective other aspects of our strategy may be, terrorists will continue to operate and act against our interests. The terrorist threat can never be reduced to zero, and the growing tendency toward action by small, ad hoc groups—freelance terror—holds the potential for significant numbers of incidents with only a loose motivational link. Under these conditions, U.S. and allied policy will need to hedge against continued terrorism, limiting its scale and destructiveness, as outlined below.

• *Harden key policies and strategies against terrorist interruption.* Beyond hardening key civilian and military facilities, the United States must consider ways of hardening policies to limit terrorist risks to our national interests. Key negotiations, such as the Middle East peace process, might be put on a faster track to reduce the opportunity for extremists to disrupt the process through terrorism. Various operations other than war, especially peacekeeping deployments, might be timed and configured to reduce the potential for terrorist attacks on U.S. forces (e.g., without a prolonged and uncertain exit phase that makes terrorism an attractive option for elements aiming to end a deployment).

---

[91]See Chapter Three.

• *Emphasize stand-off and space-based capabilities for presence and intervention in the most chaotic and unstable regions.* In addition to moving toward an expeditionary approach to power projection as a means of shaping the strategic environment, U.S. and USAF strategy can hedge against terrorist risks stemming from anarchy and regime instability by emphasizing long-range strike and space-based surveillance as a contribution to regional security. Soldiers and aircraft on the ground, in-country and vulnerable to terrorist attacks, should not be the only measure of our security interests and commitments, although in some cases an in-theater presence will remain essential for deterrence and reassurance.

• *Prepare to mitigate the effects of conventional and unconventional terrorism.* The difficulty of eliminating the terrorist risk—regardless of national strategy—and the growing lethality of international terrorism point to a need for measures and capabilities aimed at limiting the consequences of terrorist incidents. The trend toward fewer but more spectacular attacks means that special operations forces for intervention and hostage rescue will be a vital "force in being," if infrequently employed. In fact, hostage rescue, a traditional raison d'être for antiterrorist forces, may be a declining mission as politically motivated terrorist groups with explicit agendas give way to religious, millenarian, and "asymmetric" terrorists with less finely calibrated and more destructive agendas. Special operations forces are likely to be employed in the future for forcible apprehension, or for preemptive action, especially where agents of mass destruction are involved.

The potential for highly destructive and disruptive terrorist attacks in urban areas, possibly with weapons of mass destruction, has encouraged more active efforts to prepare municipalities in the United States and elsewhere to recognize and respond to such attacks. In the wake of the Aum cult's chemical attack in the Tokyo subway and revelations about planned attacks by Islamic extremists on targets in New York, and many other minor incidents involving agents of mass destruction, this emphasis is likely to continue and deepen. Policymakers and publics may eventually come to regard this as the leading post–Cold War civil defense issue. Civilian agencies are not yet well prepared to detect and manage the consequences of a disastrous chemical, biological, or radiological attack, not to mention the detonation of a nuclear device—although they are improving.

Addressing these issues will be a fertile area for cooperation between civilian and defense agencies, as well as the military services, and a growing source of demands for operations other than war.

In the realm of information operations, the United States and the USAF must weigh carefully the implications of modernization and the growing connections between military and civilian infrastructures. In some cases, we may wish to pay a price in terms of efficiency to harden and insulate critical communications links.

CONCLUSIONS

Overall Observations

Most contemporary analyses of terrorism focus on terrorist political violence as a stand-alone phenomenon, without reference to its geopolitical and strategic context. Similarly, counterterrorism policy is rarely discussed in terms of its place in broader national security planning. Prior to the specter of "superterrorism" using weapons of mass destruction, terrorism, however horrible, never posed an existential threat to U.S. security. With the important exception of WMD, terrorism still does not pose a grave threat to America's future as it does to many other societies around the world. But many types of terrorism do pose a threat to U.S. interests, from homeland defense to regional security and the stability of the international system. As a global power, the U.S. perspective on terrorism is bound to differ in substantial ways from that of others, including allies such as Britain, France, and Israel, whose experiences provide lessons, but not necessarily direction, for U.S. counterterrorism policy. In light of the preceding analysis, and other RAND research, certain overall conclusions stand out:

- *Terrorism is becoming a more diverse and more lethal problem.* Contemporary terrorism occupies an expanded place on the conflict spectrum, from connections to drug trafficking and crime to its use as an "asymmetric strategy" by state and non-state adversaries in a war paradigm. For a variety of reasons, primarily the rise of religious and millenarian groups with transcendent agendas but also the hardening of established political groups, terrorism has become more lethal. With the potential for catastrophic terrorism using weapons of mass destruction, lethality could increase dramatically.

- *The geopolitics of terrorism are changing.* Over the next decades, the prevailing image of terrorism affecting U.S. interests as a problem emanating largely from the Middle East is likely to be overtaken by a more diverse set of risks. The Balkans, the former Soviet Union, and Latin America are set to emerge as significant sources of terrorism aimed at or affecting U.S. civilian and military activities. Moreover, the vast bulk of global terrorism will continue to be confined within the borders of affected states. More anarchic futures in the Third World could fuel this type of terrorism, threatening America's systemic interests as a global power and placing constraints on our international engagement.

- *Much counterterrorism experience is losing its relevance in light of the "new" terrorism.* Many established images of counterterrorism policy, above all the use of force against state sponsors, are losing their relevance as traditional forms of terrorist behavior and organization—largely a product of the ideological and national liberation movements of the 1960s–1980s—give way to new patterns. The new terrorism often lacks a detailed political agenda against which the use of violence can be calibrated, and is therefore more lethal. It is less hierarchical in organization, more highly networked, more diffuse in membership and sponsorship, and may aim at disruption as well as destruction. The absence of clear-cut sponsorship, above all, will complicate the task of deterrence and response. It will also compel a reorientation of policy to target nonstate sponsors and individual suspects.

- *Foreign experts see U.S. exposure increasing but view the problem in narrower terms.* A survey of expert British, French, and Israeli perspectives yields a gloomy outlook with regard to U.S. exposure to terrorist risks, which are widely seen as deepening, particularly with regard to U.S. forces in the Gulf. Policymakers and observers in these allied countries are not surprisingly focused on specific national risks, few of which are analogous to risks facing the United States at home and abroad. With the limited exception of France, which shares a global and expeditionary outlook in strategic terms, terrorist challenges are generally viewed in narrower, but starker, terms. Notably, experts in all three countries share a degree of skepticism about technology as a "solution" in counterterrorism.

- *A comprehensive counterterrorism strategy should have core, environment shaping, and hedging components.* Treating terrorism as one of many national security challenges suggests a multidimensional approach. Core, longer-term strategy must address the political, economic, and social roots of international terrorism, make deterrence relevant to nonstate actors as well as state sponsors, and reduce the risk of truly catastrophic terrorism using weapons of mass destruction. The environment shaping aspect aims to create conditions for successfully managing terrorist risks: making terrorism more transparent, shrinking "zones of chaos," harnessing key alliances to the counterterrorism effort, reducing U.S. exposure, and cutting off terrorism's resources. Finally, the United States can hedge against inevitable terrorism by hardening policies as well as targets, and preparing to mitigate the effects of increasingly lethal terrorist acts.

Implications for Military Strategy and the U.S. Air Force

In many instances, air and space power will not be the best instruments in the U.S.-counterterrorism arsenal, and air power will rarely be used independently against terrorism. However, air and space power can play a role in intelligence and covert action. There will also be instances, as in the past, where air and space power will be instruments of choice in the fight against terrorism. Moreover, terrorism and counterterrorism policy are changing in ways that will significantly affect the future contribution of air- and space-based instruments.

- *Events in Sigonella and Afghanistan as well as Operation El Dorado Canyon may be key models for the future.* Air power in the service of counterterrorism will include, but will also go beyond, the surveillance and punishment of state sponsors. Deterrence and response will likely evolve in the direction of a more "personalized" approach, emphasizing the monitoring and attack of key nodes in terrorist networks and the forcible apprehension of terrorist suspects—with or without the cooperation of local states. Future demands on air power may be driven as much by requirements for intercepting and extracting suspects as by the need to attack terrorist training camps and strike regimes supporting the export of terrorism.

- *Air and space power will help make terrorism—an inherently amorphous phenomenon—more transparent.* The ability to identify and to target terrorist-related activity and to help expose terrorism and its sponsors for policymakers and international opinion will be key contributions of air- and space-based assets. As terrorism becomes more diffuse and its sponsorship increasingly hazy, finding the "smoking gun" will become more difficult but essential to determine strategies and build a consensus for action. Space-based sensors, surveillance by UAVs, and signals intelligence (SIGINT) will facilitate the application of air power and other instruments in the service of counterterrorism.

- *Gaining leverage in addressing the new terrorism will be a key strategic and technical challenge.* Future requirements for counterterrorism will be part of a broader need to tailor air and space power to challenges posed by nonstate actors, including networks of individuals. At the same time, policy instruments, including air and space power, will need to concentrate on detecting and preventing the use of weapons of mass destruction by terrorists—whether as a stand-alone apocalyptic act or as a low-tech delivery system in the hands of adversaries.

- *Much terrorism—and counterterrorism action—will focus on urban areas, with strong political and operational constraints.* Terrorism is increasingly an urban phenomenon, worldwide. One explanation for this is that the political fate of most modern societies is determined by what happens in cities. Terrorists seeking to influence political conditions have many incentives to attack urban targets. Terrorists with transcendental objectives will, similarly, find symbolic and vulnerable targets in urban settings. The use of air power in a counterterrorist mode faces the more general problem of operating in an urban environment (the difficult Israeli experience in Beirut and south Lebanon is instructive). Terrorists and their facilities will be difficult to locate and target. Operations against them or to rescue hostages will pose severe challenges for the use of air power, not least the risk of placing uninvolved civilians in harm's way. The viability of air power as an instrument in such settings may depend on the capacity for discriminate targeting and the use of less-than-lethal technologies.

- *Air power's pervasiveness and speed are advantages in the face of transnational and transregional terrorism.* In an era in which terrorist acts may take place across the globe and where sponsors cross national and regional lines, counterterrorism strategies will become "horizontal" in character. Where terrorists and their sponsors can be identified and attacked with purpose, the global sight and reach of air- and space-based assets will be valuable to national decisionmakers.

- *Air and space power will have a synergistic effect with other counterterrorism instruments.* Air and space power can be used in concert with covert action, diplomacy, economic instruments, and joint military operations. The notion of "parallel warfare," developed in relation to attacks on infrastructure in war, will also be relevant to counterterrorism operations. Operations using a range of instruments can be designed to act, in parallel, on terrorist supporters, terrorist infrastructure and networks, and the terrorists themselves.

INDEX

Abu Abbas, 21
Abu Nidal Organization (ANO), 8, 10, 21, 58–59
Achille Lauro, hijacking of, 59, 113, 137
Action Direct, 92
Afghanistan, 130, 134, 142
Afghan resistance fighters, 60–63, 65, 70, 105, 107
Africa, 106, 110
    central, 93, 100
    sub-Saharan, 93, 99, 101
Air expeditionary forces, 75, 136
Air Force barracks bombing. *See* Khobar Towers bombing
Air Force federally funded research and development center (FFRDC), xvi
Air France hijacking, 18
Airliners
    bombed, iv, 14n, 28
    hijacked, iii, vi, 18, 114
Air power, 112, 127–128, 130, 134, 142–144
al-Dawa, 17n
al-Gama'a al-Islamiya, 17n, 60
Algeria, 18–19, 21n, 27, 55, 60, 93, 109, 117–120, 132
All-channel networks, 49–51
Allied perspectives
    on counterterrorism, 135–136
    on terrorism, 124–126
Al-Qaeda, 62
Amateur terrorists, 43–44
    part-time, 21
    proliferation of, 1–2, 20–24, 37
    religious fanatics as, vi, 9–10
    as "surrogate warriors," 15
    variety of, viii, 10
America, groups within, 47

American security interests, iii, 127
    in embassies, ix
    neglected dimensions of, 5
    protecting, 35–38, 61
Analysis. *See* Terrorism research
Anarchy, 104, 109
Antiterrorism
    developing standards for, 81
    strategies for, 74
Arafat, Yasser, 57
Armed Islamic Group (GIA), 18–19, 21n, 27, 60, 62–63, 66, 118
Arquilla, John, vi, 4, 39–84
Ashara, Shoko, 20–21n
Asia, 47, 99, 110
Assassination, 131n
Asymmetric strategies, 94–96, 110
Attacks. *See* Terrorist attacks
Aum Shinrikyo sect, 13, 18, 20n, 40, 71, 101–102, 139
Autocracies, democratizing, 55

Bader-Meinhoff gang, 92
Balkans, The, 93, 100, 102n, 107, 141
Basing. *See* Continental United States (CONUS) basing
Basque Homeland and Freedom movement (ETA), 100
Basque separatist group (ETA), 8
Behavioral analysis, techniques for remote, x
Beirut International Airport bombing, 14–15n
bin Laden, Osama, 9–10, 20n, 45, 56, 58, 61–63, 70, 107, 113, 124
Biological weapons, x–xi, 38, 94, 139
Black market. *See* Weapons
Black September terrorists, iii
Blending offense and defense, 53–55
Bloodthirstiness. *See also* Lethality
    increasing, x, 38n
Blurring offense and defense, 53–55
Bombay bombings, 17–18, 27

NOTE: *f* = figure; *n* = note; *t* = table.

Bombings, 27n. *See also* Car bombings;
    Embassy bombings; Nuclear weapons;
    individual incidents
Bomb-making, 32–33
    availability of instructions, 20, 66
    availability of materials, 23–24, 29–30, 37
Bosnia, xiii, 94, 100–101, 108, 133
Brock, Peter-Juergen, 26
Bush, President George, 108

Cabinet Committee to Combat Terrorism, iii
Capone, Al, 47
Car bombings. *See also* Bombay bombings
    assessing risk of, ix
Caribbean, 92, 106
Carlos, 21
Carr, Caleb, 44, 69
Caucasus, The, 93, 99, 107
Cellular structure, 51n
Cellular telephones, 52
Central Intelligence Agency (CIA), 56
Centre for the Study of Terrorism and Political
    Violence, 10n
Chain networks, 49–50
Chechen separatists, 96, 100–101
Chemical weapons, x–xi, 38, 94, 139. *See also*
    Tokyo subway gas attacks
China, 93, 97, 103
Christian Patriot movement, 47
Civilian targets, 4, 89
Civilizational frictions, 104
Civil liberties, xi
Civil wars. *See* Lebanon
Claims of responsibility, decreasing, 27–28
Clinton, President William, 61, 70, 113
Coercive-diplomacy paradigm for terrorism,
    68–69
Coherence, 50–51
Cold War, 37, 96, 103
Colombia, 55, 92, 105–106
Committee for Safeguarding the Islamic
    Revolution, 17
Communications
    dense, 50–52
    direction of, 48, 52
Communications nodes, not modernizing all,
    77, 81
Communications technologies, 52
Communitarianism, 104
Computer conferencing, 52
Conflicts. *See also* Major theater wars (MTW);
    Small-scale contingencies (SSC)
    high-intensity (HICs), 46
    information revolution impact on, 45–46
    low-intensity (LICs), 46, 116

nonmilitary modes of, 46
resolving, xiii
spectrum of, 97–99
Confrontations with the United States, losers
    in, 108–109
Consequences of terrorism, 93–96
Continental United States (CONUS) basing
    deficiencies in, 76–77
    increasing reliance on, 75–77, 81–82
Core counterterrorism, 5
Corsican separatists, 117, 119
Counterleadership strategies, 80
Counternetwar, 55–56
Counterterrorism missions, 111–126
    of France, 117–120
    of Israel, 59, 62n, 66, 120–124
    of the United Kingdom, 115–117
    of the U.S. Air Force, 78–79, 83t, 111–115
Counterterrorism policy, 113–114, 123
Counterterrorism strategies, 74, 81, 126–140
    conceptualizing, 5, 126–127
    cooperative, 135
    coordinating in the United States, iii, xiii,
        111–115
    core, 127–133
    developing intelligence requirements for,
        82–83
    electronic, 32–33, 123n
    future of, 110–111
    growing prominence of, 99
    hardening, 138
    hedging, 138–140
    information-intensive, 5
    proactive, 77–80
    revising, 87
    technology curve for, 5, 36
    thwarting, 65–66
    traditional, 83, 87, 141
Countries. *See* individual regions and
    countries
Couriers, 53
Crackpots. *See* Psychotic individuals
Crime. *See also* Transnational criminal
    organizations (TCOs)
    nonmilitary modes of, 46
    and terrorism, v, xii, 105–108
C2 nodes, 77, 80
Cuba, 47, 103
    a terrorism sponsor, 14
Cyberwar, vi, 31, 46–47. *See also* Netwar
"Cybotage," 71
"Cyboteurs," 48
Czechoslovakia, source of Semtex-H plastic
    explosive, 37

Deaths. *See* Fatalities
Decentralization, 61*n*, 62
Decisionmaking, using information to
    improve, 46
Deep underground (DUG) facilities, 79
Defense Science Board, 2
Defensive strategies, 74
Delivery systems, low-tech, 94
Democratic Front for the Liberation of
    Palestine (DFLP), 58–59
Deniability, 44
Desert Shield, 133
Destabilization, 124*n*
Destruction, 41
Deterrence, 129–132
Dhahran, Saudi Arabia. *See* Khobar Towers
    bombing
Diplomatic tools
    coercive, 44, 78–79
    increasing effectiveness of, xiii
    sophisticated, xiv
Direct threats to U.S. interests, 88–92
Disruption, 3–4, 41, 71. *See also* Mass
    disruption
    psychological, 46
Domestic terrorism, 87–88, 99
Drug trafficking, 55
    proceeds for terrorism, 98

Eastern Bloc countries, 38
Eastman Chemical Company, 49
Economic payoffs, xiv
Economic reform, 128
Ecuador, 106
Egypt, 19, 60, 101, 103
Egyptian Islamic Group (IG), 58, 62–63
Electronic bulletin boards, 65
Electronic mail, 52, 65–66
"Emanations," reading, 83
Embassy bombings, 1, 3, 7, 9, 19, 36, 58, 70, 86
Encryption, advanced, 44
Environmental shaping counterterrorism, 5
ETA. *See* Basque Homeland and Freedom
    movement
"Ethnic cleansing," vii, 100
Ethnic separatism. *See* Separatist movements
Ethno-nationalist terrorist movements, 8–9,
    36, 48, 72
Europe, 102. *See also* Western Europe

Falklands War, 73
Fatah Revolutionary Council, 95
Fatalities, 61. *See also* Lethality, increasing
    increasing, 7
Fatwa, 10, 20*n*

Fax machines, 52
Fertilizer bombs, 29
Fidelistas, 47
Fissile materials, proliferation of available, 30,
    38
Force, threat of. *See* Military power
Force multipliers, 15
Force protection, 31–35, 72, 75–77
Force protection mission, 83
Forward basing, shift away from, 75–76
France, 141
    terrorism in, 117–120
Fundamentalist movements. *See* Religious
    terrorism
Funding, targeting, 137–138

Gamat al-Islamiya, 19
Game analogies, 46
Gangsta Disciples, 47
Gas attacks. *See* Tokyo subway gas attacks
Geopolitics of future terrorism, 99–110, 141
George, Alexander, 69
GIA. *See* Armed Islamic Group (GIA)
Global Jihad Fund, 66
Global terrorism. *See* Transnational risks
Great Britain, terrorism in, 115–117
Groups. *See* Terrorist organizations
Guerrilla warfare, iii
Gulf War, 94–95, 108, 125

Habash, George, 58
Hackers, vi
Hamas, 17*n*, 21, 47, 56–57, 80
    structure of, 61
    suicide attacks by, 1, 19, 60
    use of technology by, 65–66
Hardening targets, 114, 136
Havel, Czech President Vaclav, 14*n*
Hedging counterterrorism, 5
Hierarchies
    difficulty fighting networks, 55–56
    information, 4
    shift away from, 56–57, 67*n*
High-energy radio-frequency (HERF)
    weapons, 82
High-intensity conflicts (HICs), 46
High-power microwave (HPM) weapons, 82
Hijackings, iii, vi, 59
Hizbullah, 9, 20*n*, 58, 60, 62
Hoffman, Bruce, vii, 4, 7–38, 43
Homeland defense, 5, 89
Hostage incidents, viii–ix
Humint, virtual, 82–83
Huntington, Samuel, 104–105
Hussein, Iraqi President Saddam, 95, 125, 133

Identity. *See* "Security of identity"
Ideological clashes, 90, 99, 110
    new, 103–105
Iklé, Fred, 43
India, 102
Indirect threats to U.S. interests, 92–93
Industrial sabotage, ix
Information-age terrorism, 39–84, 95–96
    and the U.S. Air Force, 72–81
Information hierarchies, 4
Information networks, attacks on, vi, x, 2
Information revolution
    impact on nature of conflict, 45
    strengthening network forms of
        organization, 45
Information technology (IT), 52
    use by Middle East terrorist organizations,
        64–67
Information warfare (IW), 4, 31, 44, 80–81. *See
    also* Cyberwar; Netwar
Intellectual property, 48
Intelligence-gathering, xi, 74, 125
    developing requirements for, 82–83
    national technical means (NTM) of, 79
Intelligence-gathering mission, 83
Interagency networking, 55–56, 82
Interdiction and strike mission, 83
International community, view of terrorism, v
International legal constraints, on data
        "snooping," 83
International terrorism. *See also* Domestic
        terrorism
    defining, vi–vii
    making more transparent, 134, 143
    trends in, 10–12
Internet, 53
    difficulty monitoring, 65–67
Internet Relay Chat (IRC) links, 67n
Interorganizational networks, creating, 41–42
Interservice networking, 82
Iran, a terrorism sponsor, 8–9, 14, 35, 37, 58,
        102–103
Iraq
    in Gulf War, 95–96
    a terrorism sponsor, 14, 35, 37, 89, 102, 108,
        129–130, 134
Ireland. *See* Northern Ireland
Irish Republican Army (IRA), 8, 9n, 16n, 26, 29,
        36, 39, 92, 100, 115–117
    funds from drug smuggling, 98n
    targeting British forces, 31–33
Islamic Gateway, 66
Islamic Group (IG). *See* al-Gama'a al-Islamiya
Islamic Jihad, 9–10. *See also* Middle East
Islamic Liberation Party (ILP), 63

Israel, 94
    military strikes by, 79n, 143
    terrorist attacks against, iii, 1, 92
Israel Defense Forces, 60

Jammu and Kashmir Liberation Front, 17n
Japan, 92. *See also* Tokyo subway gas attacks
Japanese Red Army terrorists, iii, vi, 8, 10, 24n,
        92
Jenkins, Brian, iii–xiv, 10n, 69
Jewish community center bombing, 28
Jewish extremists, 19
Jewish Sicarii Zealots, 68–69

Kansi, Mir Aimal, 113
Kaplan, Robert, 93
Kashmir, 97, 101
Kashmiri rebels, 17n
Kenya, embassy bombing in, 1, 3, 7, 9, 19, 58,
        86
Khobar Towers bombing, 1–2, 7, 15n, 19, 58,
        61, 86, 90
Kidnapping diplomats, iii, viii
    Aldo Moro, iv
Kikumura, Yu, 24n
Killing, growing skill in, 14
Kneisel, Paul, 53n
Korea. *See* North Korea
Ku Klux Klan, 47
Kurdish region, 97
Kurdistan Workers Party (PKK), 92, 98n, 102
Kuwait, 76

Laqueur, Walter, 43–44, 102
Latin America, 92, 101, 106, 110, 141
"Leaderless resistance," 51n, 56n, 57, 138
Lebanon, 135
    civil war in, vii, 9, 122–123
Leftist organizations, 8
Leninist movements. *See* Marxist-Leninist
        movements
Lesser, Ian O., iii, xii, 1–5, 85–144
Lethality, increasing, vii, 3, 7, 10–28, 71–72,
        133, 140–141
    and decreasing claims of responsibility,
        27–28
    and greater access to weapons, 14
    and growing professionalism among
        terrorists, 25–27
    and growing skill in killing, 14
    and increasing state support, 14–15
    and need for publicity, 13, 40
    and proliferation of amateurs, 1–2, 20–24
    and religious imperatives, 15–20

Libya, 112–113
   a terrorism sponsor, 8, 14, 35, 37, 58, 89, 129–130
Lod Airport massacre, iii, vi
Logistics. *See* Terrorist tactics
Losers in confrontations with the United States, 108–109
Low-intensity conflicts (LICs), 46, 116
Lunatics. *See* Psychotic individuals

Mafia, 47
Major theater wars (MTW), 74
Maoist movements, 8
Marine barracks bombing, 14–15n
Maritime pirates, 48, 98
Maritime prepositioning of forces, 76–77n
Marxist-Leninist movements, 8, 43, 47, 58
Mass destruction, weapons of, 2, 36
Mass disruption, vi, 3
McVeigh, Timothy, 13
Medecins Sans Frontieres, 119
Mexico, 47, 55, 92, 103, 106
Middle East terrorist organizations, iii, 4, 35, 39, 47
   and netwar, 56–68
   structure and actions of, 58–64
   and use of information technology, 57, 64–67
Migrants, 48
Military forces, protection of, 31–35, 72, 75–77
Military power, xv
   alternatives to, 105
   application of, xiv, 44
Military targets, 4
Militia movements, 90
Millennialist movements, 71, 85n, 101, 140
Ministry of Defence (MoD), 32–33, 116
Mobile, large islands (MOLIs), 76–77n
Mortality. *See* Fatalities
Motivations of terrorists. *See* Terrorists
Mubarak, Egyptian President Hosni, 61
Mujahideen, 41, 45
Multijurisdictional cooperation, 55
Multinational corporations, 106
Multi-organizational networks, 45
Muniz Air National Guard Base, 34
Muslim Parliament, 67n

Narco-terrorism, 105
Nationalist terrorist movements, 50, 99–102.
   See also Ethno-nationalist terrorist movements
National Security Council, 2
National technical means (NTM), 79

Nations. *See also* individual regions and countries
   new and would be, 38
Nerve gas. *See* Tokyo subway gas attacks
Netanyahu, Israeli Prime Minister Benjamin, 97
Netwar, x, 4, 39–84
   actors in, 48–53
   background of, 45–56
   defined, 41–42, 46–48
   evolution toward, 41
   in Middle East terrorism, 56–68
   paradigms for, 71–72
   spread of, 54
Network design, 51
Networks, 39–84. *See also* Swarming
   to fight terrorism, 41–42, 82
   fully interconnected, 52
   in the future of terrorism, 41, 45
   versus hierarchies, 45–46, 55–56
   hybrid, 50
   interoperable, 41, 45
   mastering form of, 55–56
   multi-organizational, 45, 57
   organizational, 45–52, 64
   role in the new terrorism, 87
   types of, 49
New-world paradigm for terrorism, 71
New York City. *See* World Trade Center bombing
Nihilist objectives, 43, 111
Nixon, President Richard, iii
Nongovernmental organizations (NGOs), 55, 106, 119
Nonstate-actor networks, 45–46, 48
North Atlantic Treaty Organization (NATO), 92, 135
Northern Ireland, xiii, 115
North Korea, a terrorism sponsor, 14, 35, 37, 102–103
November 17 (group), 92
Nuclear weapons, 94, 139. *See also* Psychotic individuals; Weapons of mass destruction (WMD)
   dirty, 91n
   place in public culture, x
   smuggled, 107
   threat of, ix

Oklahoma City bombing, 1, 13, 18, 21n, 27, 36, 86, 90
Olympics, terrorist attacks at Munich, iii
Omnibus Terrorism Act of 1986, 113
Operational decentralization, 61n
Operation El Dorado Canyon, 112, 116, 142

Operations other than war (OOTW), 46
Organic structure, 48–49
Organizations. *See* Terrorist organizations
Osirak, air raid on, 79n
Overreaction, factors increasing likelihood
    of, xi

Pakistan, 60
Palestine, 95, 101
Palestine Islamic Resistance Movement. *See*
    Hamas
Palestine Liberation Front (PLF), 58–59, 95
Palestine Liberation Organization (PLO), 16n,
    21, 47, 57–58, 122
Palestinian Islamic Jihad (PIJ), 58, 60–62
Pan Am 103, 14n, 28, 37, 90, 112
Panama, 106
Parallel warfare, 144
Patterns of Global Terrorism 1996, 12
Payoffs, xiv
Peacekeeping deployments, 138
Perception management, emphasized by
    adversaries, 46
Persian Gulf region, 76
Peru, 106–107
Philippines, 61
Pirates. *See* Maritime pirates
Plastic explosive, 14, 29–30
Plots to carry out terrorist actions,
    prosecuting, xi–xii
Policy considerations. *See also*
    Counterterrorism policy
    for the U.S. Air Force, 81–84
Political deterrence mission, 83
Political payoffs, xiv
Political reform, 128
Political violence, ameliorating systemic
    origins of, 127–128
Popular Front for the Liberation of Palestine
    (PFLP), 58–59
    General Command (PFLP-GC), 58–59
Post–Cold War era, 38, 96, 99–100, 132, 135,
    138
Post-Soviet environment, 99
Power projection, 126
Power relationships, perceptions of, 108–109
Pranksters, x. *See also* Psychotic individuals
Precision-guided munitions (PGMs),
    proliferation of, 30–31
Prepositioning of forces, 76
Presidential Directive PD-39, 131n
Proactive strategies, 74, 77–80
Professional terrorists, 1, 25–27, 43
Profiling, x
Project AIR FORCE, xv–xvi

Provisional Irish Republican Army. *See* Irish
    Republican Army
Proximate responsibility, xii
Psychological component of terrorism, v, 46
Psychotic individuals, v, viii–x
Publicity, terrorists' need for, 13, 40, 72
Pulsing, sustainable, 53

Qaddafi, Col. Muammar al, 8, 78, 112, 129

Rabin, Israeli Prime Minister Itzhak,
    assassination of, 19, 86
Radical governments, 36. *See also* individual
    regions and countries
Rage, 109
Rahman, Sheikh Omar Abdel, 20n
RAND's research into terrorism, iii–v, viii–xi,
    xv, 3–4, 91, 127
RAND-St. Andrews Chronology of
    International Terrorism, xv, 4, 10–12
Reconnaissance, 134, 143
Red Army Faction (RAF), 8, 10, 25–26
Red Brigades (Italy), 8, 92
Red Hand Commandos, 16n
Redundancy, 75
Regional rivalries, 102–103. *See also* individual
    regions and countries
Religious terrorism, 15–20, 43, 48, 55, 72, 99
    potential for WMD use, 38
    rationale for, 19–20
    rising, 15–20, 37, 101–102, 140
Remote behavioral analysis techniques, x
Research. *See* Terrorism research
Response, speed of, 78
Responsibility, decreasing claims of, 27–28
Retaliation, 40, 74, 133
Revolutionary warfare, iii
Risk assessment, iv, ix–x
    typology of risks, 5
Riyadh bombing, 61
Rogue regimes, 129
Ronfeldt, David, vi, 4, 39–84
Royal Air Force (RAF), 115–116
Royal Ulster Constabulary, 115
Russia, 96, 100
    nuclear establishment of, 38, 107

Sanctuaries, shrinking, 134–135
Sandia Laboratories, ix
Sarin. *See* Tokyo subway gas attacks
Saudi Arabia, 2. *See also* Khobar Towers
    bombing
Scenario-building, 44
Schelling, Thomas, 69
Scotland Yard, 115

Security. *See also* American security interests
    changing definitions of, 96–97
    privatization of, 97
    of Russian nuclear establishment, 38
"Security of identity," 97
Security Service (MI-5), 115
Segmented, polycentric, ideologically
        integrated network (SPIN), 52
Semtex-H plastic explosive, 14, 37
Separatist movements, 9, 36, 99–101
SFOR. *See* UN Stabilization Force
Shaqaqi, Fathi, 62*n*
Sharm al-Shayk terrorism summit, 118
Shell-Sarnia Plant, 49
Shi'a groups, 17, 20*n*
Shiite groups, 62
Sigonella, 142
Sikhs, 101
Single-issue ideological movements, 99
Sinkiang Uighur province, 63, 97
Six Day War, 79*n*
Small-scale contingencies (SSC), 74
Smugglers, 48
Social instability, 86. *See also* Mass disruption
Society, dissolution of, 110
"Soft power," 46
Somalia, 61, 63, 119
Soviet Union, former, 93, 106, 141
    networks based in, 57*n*
Space-based surveillance, 134, 143
Space power, 127–128, 134, 142, 144
Special Air Service (SAS), 115, 117
Sponsors, not identifying, 70
Sri Lanka, 97
Stalinist movements, 8
Star networks, 49–50
State support for terrorism
    increasing, 14–15
    retaliating against, 80
    shift away from, 57
Strategy. *See* Terrorist tactics
Subways. *See also* Tokyo subway gas attacks
    Paris Metro, 118–119
Sudan, 100, 125, 130, 134
    a terrorism sponsor, 14
"Superterrorism," 86, 120, 140
    reducing risk of, 132–133
"Superviolence," 43
Surging strategy, 75
"Surrogate warriors," 15
Surveillance, 134, 143
Survival training, ix
Sustainable pulsing, 53
Swarming, 53–55

Syria, a terrorism sponsor, 14, 35, 37, 58, 95,
        102, 129
Systemic terrorism, 89, 93–94

Tactics. *See* Terrorist tactics
Taliban, 63*n*
Tanzania, embassy bombing in, 1, 3, 7, 9, 19,
        58, 86
Targeting terrorists. *See* Terrorists
Targets of terrorism, 35–38, 108
    hardening, 114, 136
    information, 44, 72
    traditional, 36–37
    within USAF, 72–74
Technology of terrorism, 28–35. *See also*
        Bomb-making; Weapons
    caveats about role of, 52–53
    move to advanced, 41, 43
    spectrum-wide adaptation, 28–35
Techno-terrorism, 65
Teheran hostages, 113
Terrorism, 140–142. *See also* Domestic
        terrorism; International terrorism; Risk
        assessment; Targets of terrorism;
        Technology of terrorism; Terrorists;
        Urban terrorism
    changes in, xv, 1–5, 8–10, 42–43, 98,
        140–141
    combating, vi, xiii, 74–75
    consequences of, 93–96
    containing, 2, 126
    contemporary, 2–3, 42–43
    defining, v–vii, 11*n*, 85*n*
    funding for, 137–138
    future of, 41, 67–68, 99–110
    interdiction of, 74
    living with, 124
    means and methods, 20
    new, 39–42, 85–144
    "postmodern," 43, 101–102
    psychological component of, v
    recent views about, 42–45
    root causes of, viii
    as a strategy, vi
    symbolic, 90–91
    tiers of, 43–44
    transnational dimensions of, 88
    trends in, 4, 7–38
    unconventional, 2–3, 95, 130
    unexpected developments in, iv, vii
    universal condemnation of, v
    white-collar, vi
Terrorism research, xiii, 90
    limited scope of, 2–3

rapid obsolescence of, 2
vocabulary of, 98
Terrorist acts, nature of, v, 11n, 85n
Terrorist attacks
    deterring, 129–132
    discriminant, 8
    increasing lethality of, vii, 3, 7, 10–28
    number worldwide, 11f
    preparing chronology of, iv–vi
    "spectaculars," 12
Terrorist doctrines, 68–72. See also Ideological
        clashes
    coercive-diplomacy paradigm, 68–69
    new-world paradigm, 71
    war paradigm, 69–70
Terrorist organizations. See also Middle East
        terrorist organizations; individual
        organizations
    claiming to have bombs, x
    imperative to succeed of, 36
    most active, 57–64
    new, 9, 58, 67
    penetrating telecommunications nets of,
        83
    religious versus others, 16f
    structure of, 41, 56–57, 83–84
    traditional, 58–60
    transnational, 48
Terrorists. See also Amateur terrorists;
        Professional terrorists; Psychotic
        individuals; Training camps
    adaptability of, 37, 40
    C2 nodes of, 80
    growing skill in killing, 14
    mainstream, 36
    motives of, v, 35, 37–38, 40–43
    negotiating with, ix
    targeting, 80–81
    variety of, viii, 10, 48
Terrorist tactics
    advanced, 41
    asymmetric, 94–96
    changing often, vii, 8–10, 34n
    independence in, 57
Threats. See also Risk assessment
    direct, 88–92
    indirect, 92–93
Tokyo subway gas attacks, iv, vi, 1, 9, 13, 18,
        27, 102, 139
Tools of terrorism. See Weapons; Weapons of
        mass destruction
Training camps, 20, 143
Transnational criminal organizations (TCOs),
        48, 55, 56n, 106
Transnational risks, 2, 48, 92, 106

Trevi Group, 118
Triads (Asia), 47
Tripoli, air raid on, 78
Turkey, 92, 97, 102–103, 107
Turkish Islamic Jihad, 17n

Uighur province, 63, 97
Ulster Freedom Fighters, 16n
Ulster Volunteer Force, 16n
Underdevelopment, 110
Underground facilities, 79
United Kingdom, terrorism in, 115–117
United States
    coordination of counterterrorist efforts
        in, iii
    limiting exposure to terrorism, 136–137
    losers in confrontations with, 108–109
    terrorist threats to, iii, vii, 3, 35–38, 88–111,
        124–126, 141–142
U.S. Air Force, 35–36
    C2 nodes of, 77
    counterterrorism missions of, 78–79, 83t,
        142–144
    and information-age terrorism, 72–81
    new strategy for, 74–75
    policy considerations for, 81–84
    and proactive counterterrorism, 77–80
U.S. Counterterrorist Center, 56
U.S. Department of Defense, 10
U.S. Department of Energy, ix
U.S. Department of State, viii, 12, 62
    designation of states sponsoring terrorism,
        14
Unmanned aerial vehicles (UAVs), 83, 123n
UN Stabilization Force (SFOR), 100
Urban terrorism
    gangs, 48
    guerrilla warfare, iii

Van Creveld, Martin, 42–43
Venezuela, 106
"Virtual humint," 82–83
Virtual presence, 75
Vulnerabilities
    identifying, x, 37
    reducing, 81–82

Warfare. See also Conflicts; Major theater wars
        (MTW); Operations other than war
        (OOTW); Small-scale contingencies
        (SSC)
    a component of terrorism, xii, 41
    conventions governing, vii
    irregular, 42

paradigm for fighting terrorism, 39, 70, 78,
    82
paradigm for terrorism, 41, 68–72, 94–96,
    125
parallel, 144
rules of, v
Warsaw Pact arsenals, 38
Weapons. *See also* Biological weapons; Bomb-
    making; Chemical weapons; Nuclear
    weapons
    black market for, 38*n*, 43, 48
    conventional, 36
    economic denial as, 91*n*
    electronic, 82
    growing availability of, 14, 44
    improvising, 32–34
Weapons of mass destruction (WMD), 2,
    36–38, 69–70, 91, 132–133
    facilities for producing, 83
    growing availability of, 43
    heightened willingness to use, 71, 86–87

Western Europe, 92
What ifs, x
Wilsey, General Sir John, 26
Wohlstetter, Albert, 75
World Islamic Front for Jihad Against Jews and
    Crusaders, 63
World political system, attempts to
    undermine, 43
World Trade Center bombing, iv, 1, 13, 17,
    20*n*, 21–24, 36–37, 86–90, 108
World War II, 73
World Wide Web (WWW) sites, 52, 65–66

Yasin, Abdul Rahman, 23
Yemen, 61
Younis, Fawaz, 113
Yousef, Ramzi Ahmad, 13, 23
Yugoslavia, former, 101

Zanini, Michele, vi, 4, 39–84
Zapatista movement, 47, 55